THE ESSENTIAL GUIDE TO
EVERY KIND OF BUSINESS WRITING

The Business Writing Handbook shows you how to:

- Clarify your thoughts and then communicate exactly what you have in mind

- Improve your writing style by using strong verbs and simple, direct sentences

- Use footnotes, edit your own writing, overcome "writer's block"

It includes dozens of examples from the writings of successful business people in every profession, provides a special review of grammar and usage, including a handy list of the most commonly misused words—and much more!

THE BUSINESS WRITING HANDBOOK

THE ESSENTIAL GUIDE TO WRITTEN COMMUNICATION FOR PEOPLE IN BUSINESS, GOVERNMENT, AND THE PROFESSIONS

BY WILLIAM C. PAXSON

BANTAM BOOKS
TORONTO · NEW YORK · LONDON · SYDNEY

THE BUSINESS WRITING HANDBOOK

A Bantam Book/May 1981

ACKNOWLEDGMENTS

Illustrations of catalytic converters reprinted from Motor Magazine; *copyright ©
1974 by The Hearst Corporation. By permission of Motor Magazine.*

Bar chart and accompanying information reprinted from September, 1974 issue of
Seminar. *By permission of American Press Institute.*

Title page and copyright page reprinted from Technical Reporting *by Gould and
Ulman; copyright © 1952, 1959, 1972. By permission of Holt, Rinehart and Winston,
Inc.*

*"Power Plant Early Alert Reporting System," by Electric Power Research Insti-
tute; copyright © 1979. By permission of EPRI.*

*News release from Miles Laboratories, Inc.; 1978. By permission of Miles
Laboratories, Inc.*

Excerpt from The World Book Encyclopedia; *copyright © 1980 by World Book-
Childcraft International, Inc. By permission of World Book-Childcraft International,
Inc.*

Quotation from The Careful Writer *by Theodore Bernstein; Atheneum, 1973.*

Quotation from America's Handyman Book, *by the Staff of the Family Handyman;
copyright © 1961, 1970 by Charles Scribner's Sons. By permission of the publisher.*

Quotation from "No More Secondhand God" from No More Secondhand God and
Other Writings, *by R. Buckminster Fuller; 1963, Southern Illinois University Press.
By permission of Ann Emmons Mintz.*

Quotation from Computers in Society *by Donald H. Sanders; copyright © 1976. By
permission of McGraw-Hill Book Company, Inc.*

Proposal from The Proposal Writer's Swipe File, *Taft Corporation, 1973. By
permission of the Taft Corporation.*

Quotation from "On Societies as Organisms" from The Lives of a Cell *by Lewis
Thomas; copyright © 1971 by the Massachusetts Medical Society. Originally
appeared in the* New England Journal of Medicine. *By permission of Viking Penguin,
Inc., and Penguin Books, Ltd.*

Quotation from Writers at Work: The Paris Review Interviews, Second Series;
Viking Press, 1963. By permission of Viking Press.

Quotation from The Poetry of Robert Frost, *edited by Edward Connery Lathem;
Copyright 1930, 1939, © 1969 by Holt, Rinehart and Winston; copyright © 1958 by
Robert Frost; copyright © 1967 by Lesley Frost Ballantine. By permission of Holt,
Rinehart and Winston, Publishers.*

Book design by Kathleen Ferguson

ISBN 0-553-14344-1

Published simultaneously in the United States and Canada

PRINTED IN THE UNITED STATES OF AMERICA

0 9 8 7 6 5 4 3

CONTENTS

ACKNOWLEDGMENTS

Many people contributed samples, ideas, and advice, so many in fact that there is simply not enough space to name them all. Therefore, I wish to thank here the members of my family, who had to endure the most during the writing of the book, which took place at odd hours of the early mornings, late nights, and weekends: Diana, my wife, for typing the manuscript; Debbie, for preparing the charts and graphs; Bob and Mark, for encouragement and jokes; and Janet, for keeping me on my toes by asking, "Just what is it you do all day long?"

PREFACE

This book presents basic guidance that will help you organize and write clear and effective letters, memos, reports, proposals, technical documents, and more. These types of writing are often brought together under the term *business writing*, a collective name used to describe writing done in private industry, the professions, and government. The book is planned for the business writer who is by training or vocation an engineer, mechanic, economist, clerk, doctor, secretary, manager, executive—any specialty other than that of professional writer.

The book concentrates on the essentials of business writing and is designed to be used by the writer in frequently encountered situations on the job. It will also serve as a text for college level and adult education classes that bear titles such as Business Correspondence or Writing for Industry.

My qualifications for writing this book are derived from a career that dates back to 1966. I began not as a professional writer but as a navigation instructor who was pressed into service to write training manuals. I later acquired a master's degree in English and eventually advanced into the dual careers of editing and teaching business writing.

Along the way, I learned that business writing is at once like and unlike all other forms of writing. The similarity exists in that the purpose of all writing is the same: Inform the reader. The reader's needs are paramount, and these needs demand that we use the right word, strive for clarity of statement, and organize statements logically. The difference exists because the business writer seldom has the luxury of specializing. The novelist can become immersed for months in one long project, and the reporter can enjoy an endless variety of short pieces. But a business writer is responsible for reports and letters and memos, of varying lengths and complexities, and tables and charts and graphs. All of this must be done within the budget and before the deadline and while accomplishing a variety of other tasks.

This book is designed to help business writers cope with these similarities and differences.

You will find the book useful in whatever pattern you read it. I urge you, however, to read Section I first. Section I covers some important material about the chief character of this book: the reader. Section I also gives some suggestions about organizing and managing the task of writing. After you have finished Section I, you may pick and choose as you wish, read the book in order, or scout around in the table of contents or index for topics of interest.

Section II offers discussions and examples of the different types of business writing: letters, memos, reports, proposals, resumés, news releases, and technical writing. The examples are from the writings of successful business communicators in a variety of professions.

Section III takes on the inner mechanics of writing, the grammar and usage necessary for accurate communication. Here you will find help with picking the right word, using verbs, writing sentences and paragraphs, tying thoughts together, and punctuating your writing.

A short section (Section IV) on editing comes next. The purpose of this section is to show how to convert a rough draft into final form.

These instructions are followed by Section V, which is about the special areas of visual aids, nondiscriminatory writing, the business writer and the law, documentation, and library research. For your convenience, lists of useful publications are placed near the end of the book. One such list is in the section on library research. The other list makes up the bibliography.

Throughout, I have tried to simplify instructions as much as possible in order to make the book easy to use. The result is a general approach that will work in most cases. Still, the principles set forth here cannot possibly cover all situations, and the wise writer who has mastered these general rules will know how to handle the exceptions.

Lastly, the reading of a book on writing is but a beginning step in becoming a writer. The intermediate and final steps are a continuing mixture of hard work and practice: writing and rewriting and critical analysis and often more rewriting and editing. The work that goes into good writing makes it a solid record of what has been said or done. And writing does have the advantage of being available so that it can be edited and rewritten. The spoken word does not have these advantages.

But writing is a doubly hard form of communication because of the nature of the printed word. The printed word does not have gestures to help it. The printed word does not, like the speaker, go back and forth over difficult points. The printed word does not answer spur-of-the-moment questions. Therefore, for you and me as writers to make the printed word work, *we* have to do the work.

I.

BEFORE WRITING

Polonius:
　What do you read, my lord?
Hamlet:
　Words, words, words.
Shakespeare (*Hamlet*)

Most readers are in trouble about half the time.
E. B. White (William Strunk, Jr.,
and E. B. White, *The Elements of Style*)

I-A.

THE PROBLEM OF AUDIENCE

KNOWING THE READER

Teachers and editors spend hours lecturing writers on the need to aim for a particular reader. In high school and college writing classes, the reader is often described as "a student or teacher on this campus." Article writers study magazine styles and advertising to learn about readers' tastes and education. Novelists define their readers in terms of tastes (such as literary or popular) and genres (such as romance, western, and science fiction).

But writers in government and industry often sit at their desks pondering just who is going to read a report or a letter. We often do not have the easy task of writing for a known, narrow audience. Twin dangers exist. We can write too simply, which is not usually the case. Or we can write in a style that is so complex and gobbledygooked that no one understands us—and that is all too often the case.

As a step toward knowing our audience, let's consider the reader to be one or a combination of the following types: general public, expert-layman, or decision maker.

General public. Often you can consider your reader to have the reading level of the general public. If you take this approach, keep in mind that reading levels have been steadily declining over the past decade. You may be writing to someone who has a reading problem. You may also find that some of your readers are not native users of English. They will find it rough going in a swarm of complex constructions and long, twisted sentences.

3

Expert-layman. Each of us is an expert, but only in a certain field. In other fields, we become laymen. In any company or bureaucracy there are experts in your field. These same experts become laymen, however, when they are required to read material out of their fields.

Consider this example. If you are a soil scientist writing a report for another soil scientist, you are one expert writing to another expert: Use the vocabulary that you are both familiar with. However, if you are a soil scientist writing a report that will be read by your company's attorneys, you are writing for laymen. In this case, you will have to find a common vocabulary (or send a long a copy of the code).

It is safest to assume that laymen will read your report. It is also reasonable to assume that you will not have time to prepare two reports, one for the expert and one for the layman. Plan accordingly, and pick language that will work for the layman.

Decision maker. Perhaps your most important reader is the decision maker. The decision maker is often referred to as a manager. Other descriptive terms are: officer or executive in government, industry, or the military; congressman, senator, or cabinet member; activist, environmentalist, or lobbyist; the sole proprietor of a small business, the partners in a fashion boutique, the dairy farmer down the road, the family doctor, and more.

Good writing helps make decisions, and decision makers want to read writing that will help them act without wasting time. It is the decision maker who determines how many people are to be hired or fired and how the money is to be spent or how the budget is to be cut. To be of service to the decision maker, the writer must write in terms that are easily understood and arrange the message for easy reading and easy use.

WRITING FOR THE READER

Your reader needs to be informed, as quickly as possible, as accurately as possible. What can you do to help?

Have thoughts worth putting into print. Nothing is more important than solid content. Begin by asking yourself these questions. Should your message be written or orally presented? Is it worth presenting at all? Does some other document already cover it? Next, narrow the topic. Make this your goal: Do less and do it better. Finally, stay on the track; don't digress or ramble.

Use appropriate language. Appropriate language is plain language. Plain language is made up of the simplest word to do the job, the shortest sentence to express an idea, the briefest paragraph to explain a topic. Plain language is the language of conversation, of friendship. Plain language is direct.

To write plain language, begin by choosing the right word. Use simple words, because simple words are most easily understood.

Still, you have to use your own judgment, for the simplest word is not always the most accurate. As an example, the words *head cold* are used to refer to a minor ailment that is accompanied by a variety of uncomfortable symptoms. One of these symptoms is *rhinitis*—an inflammation of the mucus membranes of the nose. To most of us, *head cold* describes how we feel. To the doctor, however, *rhinitis* is a more accurate term.

Also, use words that cater to your audience's specific interest. Here's what I mean. I once reviewed a report in which the first sentence contained these words: "ships, boats, and their appurtenances." The report was written for sailors and operators of drydocks and shipyards. Now, seagoing folk are a proud, feisty bunch. They call a spar a spar and a boom a boom. They talk about fittings, hardware, masts, and lines—all kinds of specialized terms. But *appurtenances?* That's a lawyer's word. The writer who used it in that report lost a lot of credibility in the very first sentence.

Another ingredient of plain and appropriate language is the short sentence. In your writing, it's best to aim for an *average* sentence length of 15 to 20 words. A sentence is a unit of thought, and readers can grasp your thoughts better if you present them in short bursts. And don't worry about insulting your reader's intelligence. Short sentences make the reader's task easier, and no reader will get mad at you for making things easier.

Appropriate language also consists of headings, transitions, and paragraph topic sentences. These tell the reader where you've been, where you are, and where you're going. They tie thoughts together and smooth out the bumps.

And appropriate language also uses frequent visual aids— tables, charts, graphs, and illustrations. These add variety and can explain far more than words.

Pick the best format. *Format* means the organizational pattern of a piece of writing, the arrangement of the parts. In most types of business writing, the best format states the main idea early.

Of course, that advice is easy to say but often hard to follow, for one or a combination of reasons. First, a new or a timid writer often approaches the subject by backing into it. Second, it is very possible when you write to get totally wrapped up in what you consider important. When you do that, you may not recognize what is important from the reader's point of view. Third, college and high school composition classes stress what I call the building-block format.

The building-block format follows the form of inductive reasoning. In inductive reasoning, you gather evidence to establish a conclusion; you use known data to arrive at a new principle. When we use inductive reasoning, we follow this example:

Observation 1: The car parked by the fire hydrant has been there for several days.

Observation 2: Parking tickets are under the car's windshield wipers.

Observation 3: A thick layer of dust covers the car.

Observation 4: The car has a flat tire.

Conclusion: The car parked by the fire hydrant is an abandoned car.

Each observation by itself cannot lead us to a satisfactory conclusion, but by reasoning inductively, we can combine the observations to eventually develop a conclusion.

Inductive reasoning is an excellent way of thinking, and it helps put solid thought content into writing.

Nevertheless, formats that literally follow the inductive or building-block pattern are mystery stories. The story begins, the plot unfolds, details add up, the action rises to a climax, and finally, after two or three hundred pages, we know whodunit.

That's great for entertainment, for spicing up the odd hours of our spare time.

But the readers of business writing are on company time, not spare time. We demand to know on page one whodunit.

So the way to deal with this problem is to flip the story over. Write it down in the order that led you to your conclusions and then move your conclusions up to the front where they can most quickly serve the reader. In other words:

[Conclusion] The car parked by the fire hydrant is abandoned. [Observations] It's been there for several days, is covered with a thick layer of dust, and has several parking tickets and a flat tire.

If you have a problem doing this, try adopting the conversational approach to writing. This approach is based on the idea that you should talk to the reader as if both of you are face to face.

The conversational approach works something like this. Suppose you are inviting friends to a party. You'd more than likely say, "C'mon over. We're having a party Friday night at my place." You'd then mention a few more items like the time and what to bring and what to wear. But you probably wouldn't name the number of things you're doing to get yourself and your place ready for the party. Or if you did, you'd save them until after you'd extended the invitation. The natural ability to get to an important point quickly when we talk should be used when we write.

It sounds simple. It is. But as an editor and teacher I spend a large amount of my time moving important ideas from the end of the letter to the front, from the bottom of the paragraph to the top, as in this sample:

Dear . . . :

Yours of January 12, 1978, received and contents noted. In your letter you are asking for three copies of our report #25A, entitled ". . ." and a list of people who attended our December workshop.

Please be advised that the report was prepared by . . . of the Research Division. Copies of the report are distributed free to any citizen interested in the environment. To date the report has had wide circulation here and abroad. Our December workshop was well attended with people coming from as far as Rome.

Because you indicated an interest in these documents, I am enclosing the material you requested.

If the writer had talked to the reader, the letter would have opened like this:

Dear . . . :

Here is the material you asked for in your letter of January 12, 1978.

Necessary details could have followed that opener. However, in the interests of saving time for writer and reader, a better approach might be to let the enclosed material speak for itself.

Later chapters give more advice on picking the best format. That advice can be summarized here in these statements:

1. Separate what you learned from how you learned it. In other words, separate conclusions from methodology. Give conclusions first, then methodology.

2. Use the "Did you know?" technique. "Did you know what I learned from the financial statement?" "Did you know what I learned at the pre-trial hearing?" "Did you know what I learned from the latest series of photochemistry experiments?" Answer those questions first. Then tell how you got the answer.

I-B.

GETTING ORGANIZED

THE TASK OF WRITING

Good writing requires hard work and is a slow process:

> I operate on the theory that I can produce about 50 "finished" words per hour, 30-35 if there's a lot of legwork or research involved.[1]

> He [Hemingway] keeps track of his daily progress—"so as not to kid myself"—on a large chart made out of the side of a cardboard packing case and set up against the wall under the nose of a mounted gazelle head. The numbers on the chart showing the daily output of words differ from 450, 575, 462, 1250, back to 512, the higher figures on days Hemingway puts in extra work so he won't feel guilty spending the following day fishing on the Gulf Stream.[2]

Little can be done to make writing easier and faster. But the steps listed here can help you get organized.

1. Develop a professional's attitude. Discipline yourself to write in spite of distractions. It can be done. If you don't think so, just visit the city room of a large newspaper and watch all those writers at work, regardless of hubbub.

Provide your own motivation. Don't wait for inspiration, the right mood, and perfect health. The seemingly endless number of books in stores were not written by authors who waited for just the right moment.

Take the initiative to do any project right. Do your own research. Solve punctuation problems by looking up the answers and not by bothering the boss. Talk to co-workers about how the chain of command has liked things done in the past. Turn in typewritten drafts, not handwritten; give your boss your best product.

When you finish a report, attach all the necessary letters of transmittal, cover memos, and explanatory notes. Give your boss a complete package. You'll save time in the long run.

Professionalism also means learning to accept criticism. The criticism is most often well-intended and is meant to aid both you and your boss. But if you don't understand the reason for a comment, ask. You'll only be as good a staff member and writer as the effort you put into it.

2. Make bosses earn their salaries. When assigned a writing project, get as much guidance as possible before beginning. Write down the deadline. Find out what the subject should be limited to. Ask what should be emphasized or toned down. Learn who else besides your supervisor will read the manuscript. Determine what special features should be incorporated. Check from time to time to be certain of your approach.

Also, consult with the boss on matters of money and policy. The boss worries about money and is accustomed to thinking months or years ahead about the budget. As to policy, if your efforts lead you into areas where toes may be stepped on, get the boss aside and talk it over before you put it in writing.

3. Set artificial deadlines. If your report is due on the 25th of the month, make your personal deadline five days earlier. That'll allow time for slippage, sick leave, or an extra day off.

4. Set daily goals. Try for so many words, pages, or hours. Keep track of your output, and try to eliminate flat spots.

5. Improve your efficiency and feel better while writing by taking these steps.

   a. Take breaks. Breaks give you needed rest and allow time for ideas to incubate while you're not writing.

   b. Work on a neat desk and don't put the project away overnight.

   c. Get adequate rest, relaxation, and exercise.

   d. Don't try to write for a solid eight hours. Intersperse some other activities: research, conferences, filing.

   e. Avoid excessive overtime. It burns writers out.

6. Use modern methods. Speak your drafts into a dictating machine or tape recorder. If you're new to dictating, begin with a short manuscript and work up from there. Have your drafts

recorded on magnetic card or magnetic tape typewriters, if possible; this can help speed up the process of revising.

7. Try team writing. If you do, set two ground rules: (1) in the early stages, rule out criticism and (2) be willing to accept candid criticism in the later stages.

8. Work around snags. Snags always develop. Research material doesn't arrive on schedule. A computer is late cranking out the printout. A co-writer is sick or away on business. There's no need to stop completely for these snags. Work around them by putting the problem area aside and devoting your efforts to another part. You can come back later.

OUTLINES

An outline should be used when planning and developing a manuscript to help ensure that all the points are covered. But the outline is often abandoned as the manuscript nears completion. Then, an arrangement may suggest itself that is better for the reader. In short, outline and final format frequently are not the same.

Nevertheless, outlines are useful, and many writers use one or a combination of the following types.

Conventional outline technique.   The conventional outline is a formal framework of roman and arabic numerals, capital and lowercase letters, hanging indentations, parallel statements, meaningful headings of equal importance, and balanced division of topics. The conventional outline follows this form:

I. Growth of industry in the Southwestern United States
  A. Growth in Arizona
    1. Before 1960
    2. Since 1960
  B. Growth in California
    1. Before 1960
    2. Since 1960
II. Transportation trends in the Southwestern United States
  A. Reliance on privately owned cars
    1. Cars used for work and business
    2. Cars used for recreation and travel
  B. The shift to mass transit
    1. Declining use of cars
    2. Rising forms of mass transit

    a. Subway and bus systems
    b. Car pools and van pools
    c. Trains

The advantage of the conventional outline is that it provides a visible, systematic master plan that can be followed from the start. The disadvantage is that its rigid appearance may discourage the writer from making changes.

Checklist system.   Instead of a formal outline, a list of words and phrases can be made up to cover key points. The list need not be organized in any rank or sequence. An organizational pattern can be picked in the later stages of writing. Although lacking a prearranged plan, the checklist system is perhaps the best way to ensure that the most points are covered.

Table-of-contents method.   First, write the report, following the conventional outline or checklist methods. Then, write a table of contents. Evaluate size, balance, content, and pattern of parts. Arrange in best order. The table-of-contents method is good for evaluating organization when finished but in so doing delays organizing until the last. (Is this bad? How can you snap the pieces of a jigsaw puzzle together until you see what they are?)

A variation.   You might also try putting the outline on 3 x 5 cards, tacking the cards onto a bulletin board, and moving the cards around until the best pattern is obtained.

Best of all possible worlds?   If you do not have an outlining technique that you are happy with, try combining the checklist system and the table-of-contents method. The combination will help you present the most possible points in the best possible order.

PREPARING DRAFTS

The instructions given here are for preparing drafts only. A later section on editing gives help with preparing the final copy.
    1. Write or type on every other line on one side of the paper; double-spaced copy will allow room for minor corrections.
    2. Make minor corrections above the line.
    3. If a major correction is necessary, write it on an insert and

fasten the insert to the page. Label the insert with a letter, and key the appropriate spot on the draft.

4. When writing drafts or when making corrections, use a dark ink or pencil that can be seen easily.

5. Number pages consecutively throughout. If you add pages after numbering, go to a system of double numeration: 4.1, 4.2, and so on. To help keep drafts in the right piles, put your last name by each page number.

6. If you submit drafts to a typist, remember that typists "follow copy" and should not be expected to interpret illegible handwriting to determine the sense of what is written.

II.

TYPES OF
BUSINESS
WRITING

No man but a blockhead ever wrote,
except for money.
Samuel Johnson
(In Boswell's *The Life of Johnson*)

But all the fun's in how you say a thing.
Robert Frost ("The Mountain")

LETTERS

THE APPEARANCE OF A BUSINESS LETTER

If you do your own typing or if you send out handwritten letters, these steps will help you set up a neat-appearing letter:

1. Place the date line four to eight spaces (lines), depending on length of letter, below the letterhead or top margin.
2. Start the inside address four to eight spaces (lines), depending on length of letter, below the date line.
3. Check the address and spelling of the addressee.
4. Double-space down and begin the salutation. Abbreviate titles such as *Mr., Mrs.,* and *Dr.* Spell out titles such as *Senator, Reverend,* or *Colonel.* End the salutation with a comma (informal) or colon (formal).
5. If you use a subject or re (pronounced ray or ree) line, it can go two lines above the salutation or two lines below, either way.
6. Double-space down and begin the body of the letter.
7. Single-space within paragraphs, and double-space between paragraphs.
8. Capitalize the first letter of the complimentary closing, and place a comma at the end.
9. Indicate enclosures and attachments.

The letter in Figure II-A1 follows the full-block format. That is, every line begins at the left margin. In the semi-block format, the complimentary closing and signature block begin at the center of the page; all other lines begin at the left margin.

A sample is shown in Figure II-A1.

```
January 14, 1980


Ward Forster
Alpha Products Company
P. O. Box 0000
San Francisco, CA 94100

Dear Mr. Forster:

Re:  #15B Spray Gun

I have before me your request of yesterday for information
concerning the amount of paint that will run through our
#15B spray gun in an hour.

Because compressors differ, I cannot state the amount of
paint accurately.  The only way I can give you an answer to
your question is to run a test for you with your compressor
and our #15B gun.

I'll be happy to run this test for you at your place of
business.

Enclosed you will find brochures and specification sheets on
our products.

If I can be of any further help, please feel free to call
on me.

Sincerely,


Henry C. Williams

Encs.
```

II-A1

Another form is the indented form, in which the first word of each paragraph is indented. Choosing a form is more than a matter of taste, for the full-block layout is easier and faster to type.

SELF-ADDRESSED, STAMPED ENVELOPE

There might be instances when you consider including a self-addressed, stamped envelope (SASE). The price of postage is such that I limit use of the SASE to these situations:

1. Letter containing questions sent to an individual or non-profit group, but not companies or government organizations.

2. When the SASE has been requested.

3. In preliminary inquiries in the publishing industry. This is traditional. Once a regular flow of correspondence is established, the SASE is no longer needed.

BEGINNINGS

The standard salutation is "Dear. . . ." A first name alone is used if you're on a first-name basis. If you are unsure about how a woman prefers to be addressed, use *Ms*. When writing in the blind (name and gender of addressee unknown), I suggest beginning with "Dear Sir or Madam."

Formal salutations end with a colon; informal, a comma. How do you decide what's formal and what's informal? If you're on a first-name basis with your reader, use a comma. Otherwise, use a colon.

A special problem arises with names like Jody, Francis (Frances), and Carol (Carroll). If you are uncertain of the reader's gender, I suggest using the first name in the salutation, as in "Dear Jody."

Next, use a pronoun such as *you, your,* or *yours* in the opening sentence. Besides adding a personal touch, these pronouns draw the reader into the letter. If we have any doubts about the magnetism of this "you" approach, all we have to do is look at the mass appeal of contests, advertising, and how-to-do-it literature. Almost everything written in these fields uses the "you" approach liberally. Some sample beginnings are:

We are glad to send you the information you want on the recent change in the examination procedures for a pilot's license.

Thank you for your letter of June 19, 1979, concerning your son's insurance. We appreciate the opportunity to look into this problem for you.

Thank you for your promptness in returning our checklist file on ethics in public relations.

Your letter of June 19 proposed many interesting suggestions for marketing our new synthetic oils.

The special problem of opening sentences. In the opening sentence of an answering letter, how much of the input letter should you refer to? Answer: In your first sentence (or two at the most), restate the subject of the input letter. Use as few words as possible. Restating is done because:

- The writer of the original letter may have written several letters on the same date. Your restatement of the problem will help refresh your reader's memory and refocus attention.

- Restating the subject helps preserve the history and continuity of communication. Some day your legal department will thank you for having such a procedure.

Answering for another. How do you begin a letter that you've been asked to write for a high-ranking official? Some writers begin with "Governor Smith has asked me to reply to your letter of . . ." or "Mr. Jones has asked me to answer. . . ." If the governor or the company president has seen the letter and knows you, those are honest beginnings. In other cases, try something like these, and mention why you're qualified to answer:

> Your letter of July 1 to Mr. G. A. Angestom has been forwarded to me for reply, for I am the officer in charge of loans.

> I have been asked to respond to your letter of July 1 to Mr. G. A. Angestom, for my division deals with the maintenance of passenger aircraft.

> I am responding to your letter to Mr. G. A. Angestom, for I am the supervisor of the audio-visual library.

ADDING THE PERSONAL TOUCH

Adding the personal touch means putting back into our writing the *I*'s and *we*'s our composition teachers told us to take out. Those *I*'s and *we*'s are important. They let the reader know that a person is writing, not a machine. Very few of us have any use at all for a letter that sounds as if it comes from a machine or a computer, although computers can be programmed with stock phrases and paragraphs in order to grind out letters that sound nicer than those written by some people.

The *I*'s and *we*'s are part of a larger scheme called *tone*. Tone refers to the way the writer conveys an attitude or a mood. To break this definition down some more, here is a list of just a few words used to describe tone:

simple, direct
complex, difficult
angry, indignant
sympathetic, concerned
indifferent, apathetic
serious, solemn
humorous, funny
personal, cordial
friendly, informal
elegant, formal
stilted, pompous

The tone of a letter often determines how the reader reacts to the message. A cordial tone will draw the reader along with the writer. An antagonistic tone will "turn off" the reader. A reader who is offended by the tone of a letter may become agitated and uncooperative. Both of these are undesirable and unproductive results.

In short, tone is important and can be thought of as another form of publicity and customer relations, another way of establishing good will.

A difference in tone can be seen in the two letters below. The tone of the first letter is businesslike and firm. The second is friendlier and borders on the informal.

Dear Ms. Smith:

In your letter of January 22, 1976, you asked about reinstatement of your driver's license.

Your driving privilege is suspended under Vehicle Code Section 10000C, effective March 19, 1975, and under Vehicle Code Section 10000B, effective November 21, 1975. Both suspensions are required *by law*. We cannot shorten or change them in any manner.

While your driving privilege remains suspended, no one has the authority to issue you a driver's license for any purpose. Our Department is allowed no discretion in the matter.

As it stands now, your driving privilege will be eligible for reinstatement on May 20, 1976. To effect reinstatement, you must file proof of your financial responsibility with our Department. Proof is required through March 19, 1979.

We appreciate this opportunity to explain the Department's position, Ms. Smith.

———————

Dear Mr. Court Clerk:

We need your help.

Here's a copy of the abstract we received from your court on December 12, 1975.

We're not sure we've correctly identified it to the driver record of John Smith, D 0000.

Please send us any identifying information you have available. An envelope is enclosed for your reply.

Have a nice day.

Format.   Format refers to the arrangement of the parts, the form of organization the letter takes.

Tone relates to form. In general, you should put what the reader needs to know right up there at the top of the letter. If you haven't done that, the reader may get disgusted with the letter, you, and your company.

The results may be the same if you broadside a reader with a curt negative statement in the opening sentence: "No consideration can be given to your claim at this time." If you have bad news to put in a letter, lead up to it, condition the reader for what is to come.

In short, the proper format for a letter conveys the message most efficiently and most pleasantly.

Language.   Work on developing the conversational style of letter writing. Imagine yourself talking face to face with the reader. Make notes as you talk. Call the reader by name. Use *you, your, I, me.* Take that very crude conversational draft, polish it into good written English—in the plain style—and you have a letter.

Let's look at it this way. If you were to walk up to my desk and ask for help with a report, you'd probably say something like, "Bill, I've got a tight deadline on this report. Can you help me?" You would not say, "The purpose of this visit is to solicit assistance for the completion of report X."

I don't know anyone who talks like that, but I read letters written in that style. That kind of writing is stilted and pompous. Worse, it shows that the writer is afraid. The big words and the impersonal approach are disguises. They are masks used by people who cannot or will not make the commitment of putting even the smallest fraction of themselves on paper. And readers know that.

Here is some help.

Before starting a letter and throughout the writing of one, keep in mind that a letter is, above all else, a personal communication. Business and government letters often deal heavily in legal and scientific language, interpretations, and requirements. This type of writing borders on the formal. Still, a letter does go from one individual to another and should be written with a personal touch and in a tone that will result in a favorable response.

Keep a personal touch throughout the letter. If the letter is long, refer to the reader by name in the body of the letter. As an example, you could introduce a point by writing, "Concerning other features of your company's programs, Ms. Smith, our position is. . . ."

Use *please* and *thanks* or *thank you* where appropriate. Use contractions freely. Nothing cuts through formality faster than words like *it's, don't, here's,* and *haven't*.

Do not argue with the reader. Just supply the information necessary to clarify points that are confusing or that might be misunderstood.

When you present unpleasant ideas, use neutral or positive language that presents the situation in the best light possible:

UNPLEASANT OR NEGATIVE	NEUTRAL OR POSITIVE
Because your system failed four different tests. . . .	Because testing requirements were not met. . . .
Your company's failure to adopt Rule X will only cause continued contamination of the environment.	Early adoption of Rule X will do much toward improving the environment.
Of the 28 positions slated for reduction, we have only had to lay off 8 employees.	Of the 28 positions slated for reduction, we have been able to retain 20 employees.

Keep in mind that we are not *forced* to do anything to a person or a company. Laws and policies *require* certain actions, and there is a very large difference in meaning and in sound between *force* and *require*.

Also, do not rub on the soft soap or beat around the bush. And be sincere. Do not gush with superlatives. Do not give unwarranted praise. Do not create false hopes in the reader. Do not repeatedly take an organization to task for its shortcomings and then end a letter by saying, "I have enjoyed the opportunity to write to you," when it is obvious that the opportunity was not enjoyable at all.

Finally, if you cannot answer all of your reader's questions, supply names, addresses, or phone numbers where more information can be obtained. Tell the reader why that person can be of greater help than you.

Timing. You can do a lot for good will by solving customer problems quickly. Sometimes, though, that's not possible. The workload may be staggering, or you may be shorthanded. In that case, you can keep the customer informed:

I am pleased to inform you that your June 27, 1978, application for financing your control system has been forwarded to our division for evaluation.

Because of the nature of the application, I have assigned it to two different branches for review. If we have any questions, a member of one of those branches will get in touch with you. Also, I must inform you that our current workload is such that we do not expect to be able to begin our evaluation for four to five weeks.

In the meantime, please feel free to call me regarding any aspect of your application. My phone number is (000) 000-0000.

We do make mistakes. When an apology is in order, make it. Here are some samples.

If you feel an error has been made, Ms. Jones, please let us know. We will be glad to check further.

Thank you for advising us of the error. We are sorry for any trouble and inconvenience this matter may have caused you.

Please disregard the bill sent to you on April 4. It was sent by mistake.

Please accept our apology and our assurance that we will be more careful in the future.

Softer language. The passages in the left column below were softened and rewritten in the right column. The rewritten versions can serve as examples for putting a milder tone in letters.

INSTEAD OF	TRY
You must apply to the appropriate district for an exemption.	Only a district can grant an exemption. I suggest (recommend) you write to . . . .
It is recommended that prompt action be taken by the department to settle these claims.	We (I) recommend that you take prompt action to settle these claims.
It has been a pleasure to work mutually on this project.	I have enjoyed working with you on this project.
The return of this report, after review, is requested.	Please return this report after you have reviewed it.
In reference to your recent letter, you misunderstood the proof requirements.	Perhaps the proof requirements were not clear.
If this change is desired, it is necessary that the attached form be signed and dated.	If you wish to make this change, please sign and date the attached form.
You should write to that office as we instructed you in our letter of August 24.	Please write to that office.
You failed to sign the application.	Please sign the application.

ENDINGS

If you think your reader will have a need to get in touch with you, end in this manner:

> If I can be of further service, please let me know by (calling) (writing) . . . .

> We look forward to working with you.

> If you have any questions, Mr. Blank, please let me know.

Otherwise, just end:

> While I am sorry to disappoint you, I hope this information will be helpful in understanding. . . .

Thank you for the opportunity to review this matter (for) (with) you.

Thank you for bringing this matter to our attention.

Thank you for allowing us to clarify this matter for you.

Thanks for your help.

Thanks.

Sincerely,
   or
Cordially,

SAMPLE LETTERS

Here are a few samples that best demonstrate the practical art of letter writing and that can be used as models for the more common purposes of business correspondence. The samples vary in length, tone, and style, but a dominant theme runs through them: State the main idea early.

To ask.   Say what is wanted and why:

We are revising our in-house pamphlet on industrial safety. As part of our research, we would appreciate receiving two copies of your latest rules and regulations. Can you provide these copies?

Also, can you tell us when and if any more revisions are planned?

Make it as easy as possible for your reader to reply. To do this, you may want to include a self-addressed, stamped envelope.

To answer.   Be straightforward.

Here are the documents you requested in your letter of April 12.

If you wish any further information, my phone number is (000) 000-0000.

To invite.   Extend the invitation, provide a general description of the event, then get to the details.

It is with pleasure that I invite you to our summer session of training-for-trainers. The session will be held at the Hilton Inn North from August 1 through 4.

We have arranged a program of value to all participants. Many topics with companywide implications are scheduled for presentation by recognized leaders in the field. Ample time is allowed if you wish to participate in discussion periods. In addition, tours to two outstanding instructional materials centers have been arranged.

With your budget in mind, we have been able to establish special meeting rates with the management of the Hilton Inn North. Information on accommodations, transportation, registration, and the program are enclosed.

If you have any questions, Eduardo Chavira, session coordinator, will be glad to help. His phone number is (000) 000-0000.

To accept an invitation.   Keep an acceptance short. To avoid misunderstanding, restate the important points, but in a tactful way. Then mention any special needs.

I'll be delighted to speak at your group's noon luncheon on January 25. The theme of your meeting—"Probing the '80s"—is one I'm acutely interested in.

I'll provide my own transportation to and from the airport. I have my own screen and slide projector, but a table will probably be needed to put the projector on.

I'm looking forward to seeing you on the 25th.

To say thanks, #1.   Write it the way you'd say it.

Just a short note to say thanks for the hospitality you showed me during my visit to the Institute for the Blind. I was extremely impressed with your school. The dedication of the teachers and the enthusiasm of the students combine to provide an outstanding program.

Again, thanks.

To say thanks, #2.   A coordinator of a volunteer program wrote this letter of thanks.

Thank you for riding in the 1978 Bike Ride against Diabetes.

Thanks to you, the ride was a success! The money is being used for important diabetes education and research.

Because you collected more than $5.00 in pledges, you will be sent a free ticket for the San Francisco Giants Diabetes

Day Game. The date hasn't been decided yet—but we'll let you know.

There are still other prizes being awarded based on the amount of money collected. These winners will be notified by mail.

We look forward to seeing you at this year's ride on Sunday, October 7.

Be sure to mark your calendar now.

Thanks again!

To adjust. It is human to make mistakes, and a letter that adjusts an account or serves a similar function usually contains an apology and a statement setting the record straight.

We are sorry to learn from your letter of August 5 that you have been billed twice for treatment provided in our emergency room.

Your records are accurate, and your account does show a zero balance. Please disregard the second billing.

If we can be of any further service, please let us know.

Letter of approval. A letter of approval is most effective when it is brief and businesslike:

We have approved your application for a loan on policy #400-58-17A. The effective date of the loan is October 1. A check for $5,000 is enclosed.

Letter of transmittal. The letter of transmittal accompanies a report that you have written and are sending up the chain of command. The letter usually consists of four paragraphs:

Enclosed are two copies of a draft of my report, <u>Machine Shop Inspection Procedures.</u> The report was prepared in response to your concerns about the Chicago division, which has been receiving increasing complaints about product quality.

In the report, I recommend the hiring of an additional 100-percent inspector at the final station and the replacement of the spring installation presses on Line 3. This recommendation is based on a detailed analysis of procedures at the Chicago plant and a comparison of these procedures to those used at our other three shops.

In preparing the report, I was aided by Bill Munson, Line 3 foreman at the Chicago plant. He was especially helpful in pointing out the difficulties associated with the older presses. The suggestion to hire another inspector was proposed by Ed Garvey, of the New Orleans division.

Recommendations in the report will, I believe, solve the problem. I hope that they, and the rest of the report, meet with your approval.

As can be seen by the above sample, the format of a letter of transmittal is:

1. Open in the "Here's the report you requested" style. Give the title of the report. Mention why the report was prepared.

2. Summarize the report. Here you can take language from the report's abstract, summary, or introduction.

3. Acknowledge those who helped you.

4. Close, if you wish, with the "I hope this report will meet with your approval" style.

Contract-in-a-letter. Sometimes a contract can be written into a letter, thereby cutting down on paperwork.

As is my custom, I am sending you this letter of the financial arrangements for Susan's orthodontic treatment.

The cost of the treatment will be $1485.00. I ask that an initial payment of $450.00 be made at the beginning of the treatment. The balance of $1035.00 is to be paid in 23 monthly installments of $45.00 each. I've enclosed a series of dated envelopes for your convenience.

To keep the cost of the treatment as reasonable as possible, I do not levy finance charges, and no interest is charged on the balance due.

Items not included in the costs quoted above are cephalometric headfilm and photographs, full-mouth x-rays, and any fillings or extractions. Additional photographs and x-rays will be required after completion of the treatment. Also, I would like Susan to have an examination by your family dentist at least once every six months while she is being treated. As you are aware, regular dental examinations are essential to excellent dental health.

If you agree to these arrangements, please sign the enclosed copy of this letter and return it.

I look forward to having Susan as a patient. With her cooperation, I am confident the results will be satisfactory to all of us. I would like to stress, however, that cooperation from Susan is the most essential factor in obtaining our goal. As for my part, I will do everything possible to complete Susan's work in the shortest time possible.

Thank you for your confidence in me, and if you have any questions, please call.

Note that (1) the costs are stated early and directly; (2) there is no fine print; (3) the writer has avoided the use of legal terminology; and (4) the personal pronouns give the letter a personal touch, but the overall tone is still very businesslike. This is appropriate for what is first and last a contract.

Introducing yourself, #1.   When you start a new business venture, introduce yourself to your prospective clients. Here's one way, that of a real estate agent.

Hi! May I introduce myself? I'm Nancy England, and I've just signed on with River Valley Realty.

Allow me to give you a few reasons why you should call on me and River Valley Realty for your real estate needs.

River Valley Realty is #1 in sales in the Springfield and North Springfield areas, #1 in television and radio advertising, and #1 in billboard display coverage. We are the most productive and most visible real estate agency in the area. And, River Valley Realty offers guaranteed sales, equity advance, home warranty, trade-in, and, for your protection, quality control programs.

As for myself, I'm 32 years old and have been marketing real estate in the area for 5 years. I spent these years with the second place company, where I was the top producer for the last 18 months.

This past January, after asking many questions of a number of people both in and out of real estate, I moved over to River Valley Realty. I consider it the most professional real estate organization in the state. My second month with River Valley, I placed as one of the company's top 25 agents. In April, I was honored as the top producer in the

North Springfield office and as one of the company's top 10 producers. In May and June I was named to the President's Honor Roll of River Valley Realty.

I enjoy what I do. I feel I do it well, and I would like to help you.

So for any real estate need, please call me. Be it buying or selling, moving, renting, leasing, or just wondering about the value of your home—let me know.

In the above letter, note the strong company identification, the number of times River Valley Realty is named. Also, note that the writer is straightforward about listing her achievements. It's like grandmother said: "Don't hide your light under a bushel."

Introducing yourself, #2. Here's the way a personnel-specialist-turned-writer introduced himself to local businesses.

Enclosed is a photocopy of an article of mine that appeared in last October's Personnel Management. It's not the first article I've had published, and it won't be the last. In fact, I've been so successful with writing and publishing ventures the last two years that I've left my position as Personnel Management Analyst at Radiographics to become a full-time writer.

Writing articles on personnel problems doesn't use up all my time, however, and I'm available to take on a variety of writing chores that you might not be able to place in-house. My experience lends itself to articles, brochures, and pamphlets. I am also available to edit publications. My background is in personnel, but my writings have been in a wide variety of fields: vehicle safety, travel, recreation, and home improvement. I have a special knack for making complex subjects readable for a general audience.

If I can be of service to you, please let me know.

To notify of a change in procedure. When informing customers of a change of business procedure, (1) introduce the change as quickly as possible and (2) make instructions easy to follow.

We are making a change in our monthly payment schedule for bank credit card accounts.

The new schedule, which goes into effect with the next bill you receive, will lower your required payment from 5% of your new balance to 4% of your new balance. This means that:

—The amount you will be required to pay each month will be less than under the current schedule.

                              but

—You may still make payments larger than the required minimum amount, up to and including payment in full.

This change simply gives you the flexibility of paying a smaller amount if you so decide. If you select to pay the minimum payment under the new schedule, your monthly interest charges will be larger. They will be less if you make payments early.

So pay us according to what is best for your budget and financial situation. The choice is still up to you.

Please note that the first sentence briefly describes the change and that the customer's choices are emphasized by introducing them with dashes. These techniques make it easier for the reader to find needed information.

The art of complaining, #1.   A letter of complaint should state facts and avoid emotion. This is hard to do, for when we complain, we are often angry. The writer of the letter below— the tenant of a small, rented office—does not show anger and goes farther by using a light touch and by offering to help solve the problems.

I wonder if I could help you with a couple of problems in my office (#201)?

First, the register seems frozen or rusted shut. I think all it needs is a shot of penetrating oil and a way to get the oil up there. If you bring the ladder, I'll bring the oil.

Second, the security dead bolt needs to be replaced. Nothing is held prisoner in my office, and the whole world can get in here to see exactly what I do all day. I'd feel a lot better if a new lock was installed. I can get a trade discount on one if you can't, and I'm sure I can find time to help you put it in.

I think we've talked about these things before. No matter. You're busy, and the tinkering that I could do to help you with these tasks would be great therapy for me.

Whenever you're ready.

There are a lot of grouches in the world, and a light-hearted complaint will do wonders toward promoting good will.

The art of complaining, #2. Here's a different style of complaint:

> I received the desk set yesterday as described on the enclosed billing order. It was damaged and broken. The pen holder was completely broken off, and there are two large breaks across the base. It is definitely not in usable condition.
>
> Please advise if you want the damaged merchandise returned. If so, I will return it "postage due." However, I do not feel it is practical to pay postage on something that should be thrown out.
>
> Please ship another set as soon as possible—or advise alternatives.
>
> I suggest that if you ship another set that it be packed better than the last, or it is doubtful it will arrive here in any better condition.

I don't know how that letter strikes you, but I enjoy reading it. I think the writer has done an admirable job of controlling anger and imparting a sense of humor to the letter, all the while being firm and specific.

Resolving complaints. Here's a letter written by a consumer service representative.

> We're sorry to hear that your yogurt maker has stopped working properly.
>
> We'd like to arrange for a United Parcel Service pickup of the base section so we may investigate the problem. Please wrap the base well for protection and enclose the duplicate letter provided.
>
> There will be no charges whatsoever for this matter.
>
> In the meantime, I'd appreciate it if you would advise me of the date the package will be ready and the address where it can be picked up.
>
> I'll be looking forward to your reply so that we may make the necessary arrangements. Please accept our apologies for the inconvenience.

Handling complaints is more a matter of company procedure than of writing letters. In other words, take steps within the company to resolve the problem, and then keep the customer informed.

SAYING NO S-L-O-W-L-Y

Good letter writers generally follow this adage: "Say yes quickly. Say no s-l-o-w-l-y." In other words when writing a letter that says no, don't stage a direct assault on your reader. Put the bad news at or near the end of the message, and prepare the reader for the worst.

A pattern to follow is this one:

1. Review facts and reasons for decisions.
2. Build argument bit by bit, fact by fact, step by step.
3. Use support material to lead to a conclusion.
4. Say no.
5. Close.

If this is done correctly, the writer will develop the argument so that the reader can only acknowledge each point of evidence and the conclusion. This reduces the possibilities of further argument and more correspondence. On the other hand, letters with bad news at the beginning stand a chance of striking a wrong note on the first beat. When that happens, the reader may not read past the first sentence, and the rest of the letter is just as important.

Delaying the bad news until last is a technique taken from conversation. In most cases, when we speak to people of bad news, we usually lead up to the worst. For example, a doctor reviews the symptoms, diagnosis, and treatment before telling the patient the outlook.

Let's consider the following situation. You hire a new man who turns out to be Ivan the Terrible. During his first weeks on the job you notice that he is always late, does terrible work, makes no attempt to get along with the rest of your people, talks back to you, and drinks on the job. Now you decide to fire him. You call him into your office, more than likely do not offer him a chair, and then—What do you say?

A few bosses would growl, "You're fired! Pick up your check and get out!" Right away this opens the door to at least one question—"Why?"—and possible argument.

But most bosses would use words something like this: "Ivan, you're always late for work, I'm constantly having to have your work redone by someone else, and you make no attempt to get along with other people in the office. On top of that, you talk back to me, and, worse, I've seen you drunk on the job. I've got no choice but to let you go."

The same logic applies to letters that carry bad news. Lead up to the conclusion and condition the reader's thinking along your lines before you say no. Present your evidence first to help prevent any further argument.

Showing empathy for your reader.   One method of easing the pain of a "no" answer is to show empathy for the reader. As a help:

1. Try to find (but do not invent) something good to say about your reader. If you are writing to an officer of an industry that has taken a positive approach to your suggestions, tell your reader that you appreciate that kind of attitude. If you are writing to a person who has been particularly cooperative, send that person your thanks.
2. Acknowledge whatever problems an organization or a person may be having. If an agency is short of funds or staff, write that you understand how these shortages can hinder operations. If a company has difficulty getting a needed component, say that you realize how critical the part is. If a person is late paying a bill, say that you are aware of that person's problems. Let your reader know that you are trying to cooperate.

Let's look again at Ivan the Terrible. He's the guy we fired several paragraphs back. How could anyone show empathy for him? Well, an understanding boss might have said something like "It's obvious that routine office work is driving you up the wall" or "Maybe you have problems at home that are interfering with your work here."

In no way does showing empathy alter your decision. Ivan is still fired, the bad news is unchanged, the answer is still "No, we do not have a job for you" or "No, we cannot award you the claim you asked for."

But by showing that you understand your reader's predicament, you will make it easier for that reader to accept the bad news.

SAMPLE "NO" LETTERS

Sample no, #1. Here is a sample of a "no" letter that conforms to the pattern presented in this section.

We note from your application of September 1 that you are requesting financing for both temporary and permanent control installations. As we understand the application, the temporary installation will be replaced in eight years, but the permanent controls are designed to last considerably longer.

We can understand your desire to obtain low-interest, long-term financing for the entire modification. Certainly, the eight percent rate is more attractive than current short-term money market rates.

However, our policy is to recommend the issuance of the 30-year bonds for those control installations that are of a permanent nature only. Therefore, we can approve for long-term financing only items A and J in your application.

As to the other items, we can arrange short-term (10-year) financing at competitive rates. Or if you can alter your design to install permanent controls all around, we can then recommend the issuance of 30-year bonds for the entire project.

Please let us know as soon as possible what you decide.

Note the organization of the letter. The first paragraph restates the problem. The second paragraph expresses empathy. The third gives company policy and says no. The fourth offers alternatives. Throughout, the writer's stand is firm, but the personal pronouns put the refusal on human terms.

Sample no, #2. This letter also follows the form of the "no" letter.

Thank you for your adoption application.

The number of infants available for adoption has greatly decreased in the past few years. As a result, all state-operated adoption agencies continue to receive requests from many more families than they have babies to place. The need for homes for older, handicapped, and minority children has increased, and agencies are primarily seeking adoptive families for these special-need groups.

At the present time, we have many applications from families interested only in infants. We are therefore not accepting additional families for consideration, because we cannot be confident about placing an infant in the home within a reasonable period of time. The district office will keep your inquiry on file and will consider you along with other families when it is able to accept more families for study.

While I am sorry to disappoint you, I hope this information will be helpful in understanding the current adoption situation.

This letter shows several features worth noting. First, what is the writer hinting at? (The answer is in the second paragraph.) Also, the writer does not say no directly: The Smiths are not told that they cannot have a child; there is nothing wrong with them. Instead, the Smiths are told that no one can adopt at this time. In other words, an emotionally charged situation is handled without saying "*You* cannot have a child." It's a nice letter.

Turning down a job applicant, #1.   Telling people that you cannot give them a job is often difficult. Note how this problem is handled in the letter below. Again, the approach is, "You're okay."

Thank you for applying for the position of secretary at the XYZ Sales Corporation.

The selection of successful candidates was a difficult task because many of the applicants were well qualified, and there were many more applicants than openings. Unfortunately, at this time we cannot offer you a position.

We appreciate your interest in our company. Your application will be kept on file, and we will consider you if any opening should occur in the near future.

Turning down a job applicant, #2.   Another way of turning down a job applicant is shown in this letter:

Thank you for writing to us concerning the position of trainer. We certainly appreciated hearing from you. Although your credentials are impressive, I have decided to pursue another candidate for the position.

Please excuse my delay in letting you know, but I wanted to keep you under consideration for as long as possible. I hope you will be able to reach your job objective in the near future.

The diplomatic "no."   A diplomatic way of saying no is shown in this sample taken from a booklet called *Plain Letters*.

You make me feel very much at home in Pittsburgh. I like the people I meet there; and I am enthusiastic about the job you are doing. But I would be showing rank favoritism if I were to move to go out there to start off your Institute. I have to catch up with my obligations in other parts of the country. I am, of course, flattered that you asked me to come.

Thanks for sending me your talk on housing and recreation. It was a good piece, and I think the way you are working it out in Pittsburgh is excellent.[1]

The direct "no."   It is not always necessary to lead up to a refusal. Some business situations call for a direct "no." One is shown here.

My regrets, but I cannot complete your photo order. We have a strict organizational policy which states that photographs of employees are not available for use by news media. I'm certain you can appreciate the need for such a policy when you consider the classified nature of our work.

"No" with an alternative.   Another method of easing the pain of a "no" answer is to offer alternatives. Alternatives should be offered for two reasons: Your reader may not have thought of other options or may have thought of them but hesitates to pursue them until told to do so.

Here is one sample alternative taken from a letter in which an executive declined a consumer advocate's suggestion but proposed an alternative:

I read with interest the suggestions you offered in your letter of January 25, 1979.

As you pointed out, candy must be maintained in a clean and sanitary condition. Whether it is subjected to heat, dust, moisture, cold, or physical damage, the candy must be protected so that when the consumer opens the package, the candy is clean, wholesome, and unbroken. So far, no one seems to have developed a one-piece wrapper that will give complete protection.

As you may not know, state law prohibits any state agency from developing or manufacturing a product that would compete with the free enterprise system. Therefore, we are unable to develop a one-piece wrapper as you requested.

I noticed from your letterhead that you are a consulting inventor. Perhaps packaging is an area of research in which you could be helpful. If you could develop a one-piece wrapper which would give complete protection to the product, I would think you would have a ready market for it.

Thank you for your interest in this matter. If I can be of any further service, do not hesitate to call on me.

Use your imagination. Few "no" letters include alternatives. This is one area where the business writer can become creative and show the boss some fine thought processes.

II-B.

MEMOS

Memo is the singular short form of *memorandum*. *Memos* is the plural shortening of *memoranda*. If you look at the four italicized forms just given, you'll see that they have a lot in common with one word: *memory*. And that's how memos started out, as short notes to jog the memory.

That was five centuries ago. Since then, memos have changed a lot. More than memory jogging is accomplished by memos these days, and many memos are anything but short notes. Today, you or I might write a one-sentence memo to ask for Friday off. At the same time, a diplomat in Washington could be drafting a multi-page, confidential memo to report on a possible revolution in a politically unstable nation.

Despite differences in length and content, many memos have two features in common:

1. Distribution. A letter is usually reserved for out-of-house use, for customers and clients. A memo generally stays in-house and is read by co-workers, supervisors, and executives. Each letter you write may be read by only one person, and each good letter you write will help your company's public relations. Each memo you write may be read by many people who know you or would like to know more about you, and each good memo you write will help your reputation and promotability.

2. Ease of organization. Many offices use a form memo that has printed on it something like:

To:
From:

Date:
Subject:

It's up to you to write the memo, but the need for work on opening, salutation, and closing is lessened.

SHORT MEMOS FOR STUDY

It's essential in memos to state the purpose in the first paragraph and preferably the first sentence. Don't make your reader dig to find out what the point of the memo is. You shouldn't use stilted language like "The purpose of this memo is. . . ." Just lead off with a simple and specific statement that plunges the reader into the subject. The three memos shown here have been picked because they do just that.

1. You are an accountant. Your boss has asked you to find out the cost of a Brand X calculator. You did. You reply by memo, and you include a memory-jogger because the boss may have forgotten the request.

Per your request, I have found out that a Brand X calculator costs $49.95.

That's the important statement. It's a direct answer to the boss' question, and the answer is in the first sentence. But you may want to write more. You may want to include a *short* statement about other calculators. And you may want to help the boss decide to buy a calculator. The final memo may look like this:

Per your request, I have found out that a Brand X calculator costs $49.95.

I also learned that a Brand Y calculator costs the same and has a longer battery life.

If you'd like to have a calculator for the office, let me know which one, and I'll take care of the purchase order.

The final version may include much more information, whatever you think is necessary. But in any event, you should answer the question in the first sentence.

2. You have a middle management job. You learn that employees of another company set their own hours in a program known as *flexitime*. The switch to flexitime has reduced sick

leave usage by 15 percent in that company. In addition, a press release put out by the company says that employee morale has increased since flexitime started. You see advantages in converting your company to flexitime, and you'd like to sell top management on the idea. Your memo should open by stressing measurable benefits.

> I have recently learned that All Brands Company has reduced absenteeism by switching to flexitime. The change brought about a 15 percent drop in sick leave usage. If we were to translate a 15 percent drop in absenteeism into productivity here, it would mean an annual increase of 1,710 hours of production.

Notice that morale wasn't mentioned in the first sentence. Morale is a concept. You and I could work at the same place, and your morale could be high while mine could be low; we wouldn't agree on morale. But any number of observers using the same techniques should arrive at the same number of hours of sick leave used or hours of production lost or dollars made or saved.

Therefore, if you want to write a memo about the benefits of a program, write of the benefits in terms of numbers. Next, put the numbers in the opening of the memo.

From there you could add paragraphs on morale, how flexitime works, and your suggestions on implementing it in your organization.

3. You are an enforcement officer in a government agency, and you plan to send five members of your staff to inspect sanitary conditions at a milk bottling plant. The inspection is authorized and required by law. The inspection will last three days: March 1, 2, and 3. The operators of the plant have filed papers in court to keep you off their property. Your division chief likes to be kept informed in writing.

You have a lot of facts that could go in a memo, but what's important for an opening in this case is:

> Company Z has gone to court to keep us from inspecting its plant.

Next:

> This is an inspection that was scheduled for March 1, 2, and 3. The inspection is authorized and required by Health and Safety Code Sections 22510 through 22515.

I have directed the inspection team to not enter the plant until I have further instructions from you and from our legal branch.

What comes next? That's up to you. The specifics are down in writing and in an order that will be most useful to the reader.

A LONGER FORM FOR STUDY: THE ISSUE MEMO

Memos exist in a variety of forms. One popular form selected for study here is the issue memo.

An issue memo is written to provide executives with sufficient information so that they can make policy decisions. In order to most effectively do this, an issue memo should be brief and should present a narrow focus. When writing an issue memo, you should include discussions of alternatives and controversies. You should also have thought through the problem well enough so that your issue memo shows how much the policy change will cost in dollars and cents and what other programs the change will affect. You may want to include a section in which you list steps necessary to implement the new policy, but I suggest you ask around before you do. Some executives feel that they are being pushed into a decision when they are given implementation steps along with a new policy. Other executives expect to see these steps as part of the process.

An issue memo is presented below and is followed by an explanation of the memo's parts.

[Organization name]

Issue Memo #80-13

Division Chief	Section Chief	Originator

Subject: Board Chairman/Executive Office
(BC/EO) Route Slip

Issue: The Board Chairman and Chief Executive Officer would like a route slip designed with which they will be able to see at a glance who has reviewed material before the material comes to them.

Recommendation 1: Issue an Administrative Services Letter (ASL) to division chiefs, branch chiefs, and the Executive Office indicating flow processes for specific items (see Attachment 1).

Recommendation 2: Design a route slip to serve two purposes: (1) items routed to BC/EO and (2) items routed to all personnel. This route slip should be attached to the ASL and made into a tablet (see Attachment 2). This route slip will also eliminate the one which we are now using (see Attachment 3).

Discussion:
Background: The current route slip being used is inadequate because it neglects to show all those who have reviewed an item.

Analysis: Pros
   (1) The Executive Staff will be able to more easily see that *all* the people needing to approve a document have done so before it has ever reached their desk.
   (2) Our current route slip can serve only one function—routing material to divisions. This new route slip can serve that function as well as provide the Executive Office with information vital to the decision-making process.
   Cons
   None.

Fiscal Impact: We currently have seven dozen route slip tablets (50 pages—double-sided) in our stock room. These cost approximately 20 cents each or $16.80. There are probably 75 to 100 tablets being used currently at a cost of $15 to $20.

The dollar amount would not be significant if we ordered new route slips and recycled the existing ones.

Suggested Action Steps: We should rush order the new "Board Route Slip" as drafted on half-page tablets. Until we receive these, we should distribute copies of the new slips and recycle all current tablets.

Attachments [not shown]

The memo presented above is organized into five main sections:

1. The "Issue" section briefly and clearly states the issue or issues on which a decision is requested. This memo uses a declarative sentence, but sometimes the issue is phrased as a question.
2. The "Recommendation" section follows the "Issue" section and gives the writer's recommendation. In other words, the solution to the problem is very near the top of the memo.
3. The "Discussion" section is next. It covers the basic policy question, alternatives, and controversies. Sometimes, you may have to provide historical information here, but don't make it too involved: Most readers of issue memos are already familiar with the history of the problem. Keep the "Discussion" section as brief as possible.
4. The "Fiscal Impact" section should include an analysis of potential savings or costs. If additional costs are involved, say where the money is to come from. Include in this section an analysis of the work involved, both in your unit and in other units affected if the policy is implemented. If there are any unresolved fiscal or workload problems, say so.
5. This memo ends with "Suggested Action Steps" that present a means of implementing the new policy.

In some organizations, you will be required to read your issue memo at executive staff meetings. These meetings are attended by managers whose units will be affected by the policy change you are suggesting. These managers expect to see a copy of your memo before the meeting so that they will have time to prepare comments. To accomplish the necessary coordination, one organization follows this directive:

1. As early as possible in the development of a program change proposal (issue memo), the staff should identify other divisions whose work load will be affected by the change and inform the appropriate management staff in those divisions of the nature of the proposal. *All* proposals will be coordinated with the Management Services Division because most program change proposals affect the work load of this Division. The Division Administrator of the division originating the issue memo will be responsible for insuring that this coordination takes place.
2. Affected divisions should be given at least seven working days prior to the deadline for scheduling Executive Staff agenda items to review and comment on a proposal that affects their work load. The purpose of this requirement is to permit adequate time for divisions to define the work load effect of the proposal and to decide the manner in which it will be handled.

II-C.

REPORTS

Business writers turn out many kinds of reports. Management reports, staff reports, and technical reports are but three frequently encountered types. The different types have certain parts in common, and the purpose of this section is to provide help in organizing and writing these principal parts. The material is presented in three segments. The first segment is on the parts of a report, the second is about report formats and organization, and the third presents two sample reports for your study.

PARTS OF A REPORT

The principal parts of a report are:

- Forewords, prefaces, and acknowledgments
- Abstracts
- Summaries
- Contents lists (table of contents; lists of illustrations and tables)
- Introductions
- Conclusions and recommendations
- Support material

Forewords, prefaces, and acknowledgments. A report may have a foreword, preface, or both. A foreword is a statement written by someone other than the author of the report; the foreword concludes with its writer's name, title, and affiliation. The preface is a statement by the author of the report; a preface without the author's name following it is assumed to have been written by the report's author.

The foreword or preface gives introductory material about the subject of the report, the need for the report, and the content. Material essential to an understanding of the text does not go in the foreword or preface. This material must go in the report proper.

Acknowledgments, if few, can be mentioned in the author's preface. Otherwise, it is advisable to list acknowledgments separately after the preface. In some cases, most notably with technical reports, acknowledgments are placed after the body of the report.

As examples, the preface and acknowledgments of this book are located on pages vii and ix-xi.

Abstracts and summaries.   Abstracts and summaries go at the front of the report, before the contents list and the introduction. Abstracts are generally described as being either *indicative* or *informative*. An indicative abstract tells what topics are taken up in the report but gives little information on what the report says concerning these topics. An informative abstract tells what topics are taken up in the report and gives specific information on these topics. Combinations of the two types are possible and acceptable.

In essence, the informative abstract summarizes key content of the report. For this reason, the informative abstract is frequently called a *summary*. The result is a confusion of terms. What one organization calls an abstract someone else calls a summary, and vice versa. To find our way through this confusion and to keep matters on as practical a level as is possible, the instructions here are organized to show you how to write two forms:

• *Abstract*—meaning the indicative form that indicates what's in the report

• *Summary*—as a substitute or parallel term for informative abstract, the form that gives specific information from within the report

Regardless of name, neither form is to be neglected, for these reasons:

Today's author must recognize a second (and increasingly important) purpose of the abstract—its use in computerized

information retrieval systems. The growth of these retrieval services has paralleled the growth of computer
technology. Ulrich's periodical directory, for example, lists
over 1000 abstracting and indexing services. And, of
course, researchers are happily utilizing these growing
treasure banks of information.[2]

In addition, conference and workshop planners often use
abstracts as guides to rejecting, accepting, and scheduling the
presentations of papers and reports. What these various uses
add up to is that an abstract may be widely circulated, and that a
well-written one may generate wide interest in the report, your
work, and you.

An abstract (indicative type) of a piece of writing would be
shorter than a summary (informative abstract) of the same
piece. As examples, an abstract and a summary of this part of
this book would look like these:

ABSTRACT (INDICATIVE TYPE)

The definitions of abstracts and summaries are given, and
the uses, lengths, and techniques of writing them are discussed.

SUMMARY (INFORMATIVE ABSTRACT)

Abstracts and summaries are short versions of a piece of
writing. Abstracts and summaries are used by readers, conference planners, and in information retrieval systems. An
abstract generally indicates what is in the report, while a
summary gives detailed information from within the report.
The typical maximum length of an abstract is 150 words;
summaries are usually one to two pages long and sometimes longer. The abstract can be written based on the table
of contents, outline, or paragraph topic sentences. The
same technique can be used when writing the summary,
except that conclusions and recommendations, if any, must
also be placed in the summary.

Suggested length of an abstract. The lower limit of an
abstract is often one or two sentences. A popular maximum
length seems to be about 150 words. That's about two-thirds of
a double-spaced typed page. In any event, an abstract of a
report is shorter than the same report's summary.

Suggestions for writing an abstract.   The abstract can be written based on the report's table of contents or outline. Another method is to write the abstract based on paragraph topic sentences. If you planned your paragraphs for reading ease, each paragraph should begin with a topic sentence, a sentence that announces the subject of the paragraph. Any material necessary to support or develop that subject should be placed in later sentences. Assuming that your paragraphs do begin with topic sentences, scan the tops of the paragraphs, jot down the topic sentences, and then cut to a manageable length.

Remember also that an abstract is a self-sufficient device; that is, it must stand on its own. To do that, it should contain no references to the report's bibliography, tables, or illustrations. In addition, an abstract doesn't usually contain illustrations or tables.

One final thought: If you ever have to write an abstract of a report that you put together, get someone else to do it, if at all possible. Most writers find it extremely difficult to compress into the limited space of an abstract all of the thinking they put into the report.

Summaries.   The summary discussed here goes at the front of the report but after the abstract, if an abstract is used. Like a concluding summary, this introductory summary is based on material inside the report and is written after the report is completed. The summary is longer than an abstract, contains more detailed information, and stresses the conclusions and recommendations made in the report.

Purpose and form of a summary.   The purpose of the summary is to save time for the decision maker. A properly designed summary does this by being action-oriented. In other words, the summary leads off with or has close to its beginning a recommended solution to a problem. An outline of such a summary might look like this:

- Issue: a concise statement of the problem
- Conclusions: why there is a problem
- Recommendations: what to do about the problem
- Report highlights

The report highlights that could be included are: predicted impacts of the recommendations, limitations of the study, alternative recommendations, and names of research methods used.

Suggestions for writing a summary. When writing a summary, present the conclusions and recommendations as quickly as possible. Sometimes a list or table can be used to shorten reading time. No reference should be made to illustrations, tables, or bibliographic items in the report proper.

Suggested length of a summary. The objective is to give the busy executive no more than a single piece of paper on which actions can be based. Thus, the summary can be single-spaced or double-spaced and printed back-to-back—whatever it takes to make it fit on one sheet. Longer summaries are possible and sometimes inevitable. But you should challenge the need for them.

Abstract or summary or both? Always write a summary. In many cases, the summary is the only part of the report that busy managers will take time to read. Accordingly, a summary should be considered an integral part of a report.

As to the abstract, write it when required by company policy or requested by editors, publishers, or supervisors.

Note: Neither an abstract nor a summary should contain material or information that cannot be found in the report.

Abstract and summary: a comparison of types. Earlier I wrote that an informative abstract is sometimes referred to as a summary. Here is one such instance. In the report, it was labeled "Abstract," but it offers enough information to be a very effective summary.

This study analyzes the growth of electric space heating in the TVA region for the period of 1961 through 1974. Relatively low residential electric power rates have contributed to the present 40% saturation of electrically heated homes in the TVA region compared to less than 10% for the rest of the nation.

Disaggregated data from 144 distributors of electric power in the TVA area are analyzed by developing linear trend, logistic growth functions, and a logit model to estimate demand for electric heating and project to 1985 estimates of the proportion of electrically heated homes.

The estimated projection of electrically heated homes in 1985 based on the linear trend is 54.8%. For the logistic growth function, the corresponding projection is 57.3% in 1985. Projections based on the logit formulation, which allow the price of natural gas and per capita income as well as the price of electricity to be determinants of the proportion of electrically heated homes, were made for four price and income scenarios which gave a range of 54.6 to 66.2% electrically heated homes in 1985.[3]

This could be shortened to be the following abstract:

This study analyzes the growth of electric space heating in the TVA region for the period of 1961 through 1974. The study also projects to 1985 the proportion of electrically heated homes in the area.

Contents lists.   The contents list (table of contents, lists of illustrations and tables) shows readers where to find items in your report.

The more section headings and subheadings you include in the table of contents portion, the easier you will have made it for your readers. For instance, if you merely use the heading "Support Material" to show information from pages 6 through 28, your reader will have quite a bit of searching to do. But if "Support Material" consists of several subsections and if you list the heading of each subsection in the table of contents, you have made the reader's task considerably easier.

The contents list is not written until all pages, illustrations, and tables have had numbers assigned to them. When the contents list is made up in final form, it should be placed after the summary but before the introduction. There, the contents list will serve as a guide for the reader who has just read the summary and now wants to find pertinent parts of the report.

Introductions.   A well-written introduction will announce the report's

- Exact subject
- Exact purpose
- Scope: limits and range, detail and depth, point of view
- Plan: This is a preview, not merely a restatement of the table of contents. The preview should tell the reader how parts of the report will aid in understanding the subject.

In addition, the introduction should

- Open with an arresting statement
- Present a key idea in the opening sentence

- Provide a transition to the report's next section (often the "Conclusions")

Also, an introduction may have to

- Emphasize the importance of the topic
- Provide background, such as history, theory, or references to previous works done on the same subject
- Make policy statements as required

The introduction is often the hardest part of the report to write. It is especially hard if you try to write it before you have finished the report. The standard question is, How can you introduce someone unless you know the person? But writing an introduction doesn't get any easier if it's saved until the last. By then you are racing to meet your deadline and perhaps tired of looking at the pages stacked in front of you. What often results is an introduction not worthy of the name.

Therefore, if you are having a problem writing introductions, try this approach:

1. When you first start writing the report, draft a brief introduction. Keep the draft nearby.
2. As you write the report, add to the draft introduction from material you are putting into the report.
3. When the report is finished, go back to your introduction and rewrite it into final form.

Conclusions and recommendations. Standard to many reports are two key parts: *conclusions* and *recommendations*.

The report's conclusions answer the questions, What problem did the research solve? What are the propositions arrived at as a result of the study? Where does evidence in the report logically lead to?

Sometimes no conclusions can be reached. In that case, the reader must be told so.

The report's recommendations stem from the conclusions and are courses of action to follow. What action do you suggest to the decision maker? Is further study needed? What should be done now? Later?

Conclusions and recommendations are always written after the research is finished. However, as will be seen in the discussion on formats, conclusions and recommendations are often presented to the reader *before* the part of the report that explains the research.

Support material. Support material consists of the body of the report, the appendixes, and the bibliography. Support material usually makes up the bulk of the report and is where explanations are gone into in detail.

The body of the report is frequently divided into sections on methods, procedures, and limitations. Other topics are possible. Enough facts and data are provided to justify the report's conclusions and recommendations. The nature of the problem should be fully explained. Frequent headings and subheadings should be used to guide the reader.

ORGANIZING THE PARTS

The parts of a report can be arranged into three basic formats or organizational patterns. The terms used here are straight line, building block, and inverted pyramid.

Straight line. The straight-line format presents material in alphabetical, chronological, or numerical order or the order in which steps are to be accomplished. This format is useful for a purely informational report or for simple how-to-do-it instructions. Conclusions and recommendations usually are not part of a report based on this format.

Advantage: easy for the writer to organize
Disadvantage: can be dull reading if the style is too methodical

Building block. The building-block format opens with a brief introduction, then builds logic bit by bit, step by step, and fact by fact until conclusions and recommendations are reached. It is the type of format most often taught in composition classes.

Advantage: good for developing an argument; can be used to lead the reader to the author's desired conclusion
Disadvantage: withholds key material to the end

Inverted pyramid. The inverted-pyramid format is a type taken from journalism. In this type, the most important item is presented at the top of the story, and items of lesser importance are placed toward the bottom. As adapted to report writing, the inverted pyramid is developed in this manner. It opens with a solid introduction which is followed immediately by conclusions and recommendations. Support material makes up the remainder of the report. The introduction should contain statements that will prepare the reader for the conclusions and recommendations.

Advantage: gets to the point quickly
Disadvantage: presents conclusions and recommendations before support material is developed

In essence, the inverted-pyramid format is a building-block type with the conclusions and recommendations rearranged to better serve the reader.

The right format?   Is there a right format? In more specific terms, should conclusions and recommendations be placed at the end of the report where our composition teachers have taught us to place them? Or should conclusions and recommendations be moved to an earlier part of the report? I asked these questions of writers and executives in industry and government. Here are two of the answers.

Laura Horowitz is President of Editorial Experts, Inc., of Alexandria, Virginia. She says that they advise putting conclusions and recommendations up front, "so readers will get the point before putting the book down; to accommodate busy policy makers."

Her comments are echoed by F. F. Dietsch of the Metallurgical Research Division of Reynolds Metals Company. His organization uses this format: cover, title page, table of contents, summary, objective of project, conclusions, recommendations, method, results, discussion, and appendix. "For several years prior to issuing this procedure," he states, "each engineer and scientist used his or her own format—generally the one they used in college. This caused problems for those throughout the company who had to read them. Most are busy people who are interested primarily in objective conclusions and recommendations; thus, the format we are now using."

There is no single format that will work in all cases. But here are some guidelines that will help you pick a format.

First, remember your reader, the decision maker. The decision maker is a busy person who has other reports to read and meetings to attend. Most decision makers would rather not spend the time it takes to wade through page after page of research to get to the conclusions and recommendations. In short, you can do the decision maker a favor by putting your conclusions and recommendations up front.

Second, readers are familiar with conclusions and recommendations being placed up front. Most news stories and many popular nonfiction books are written that way. Granted, the headings "Conclusions" and "Recommendations" rarely, if ever, appear in newspapers or popular books; but that format is generally followed. Professional writers know that readers want to be informed quickly. These writers structure their work to serve readers' wants.

Third, think how you would tell a friend about your work. If the friend stopped you on the street and asked how your investigation of X was going, you would probably very quickly announce your results: "Well, what I've learned is this. . . ." Then, if time is available, the conversation might turn to your methodology. In short, the conversational approach to writing that was mentioned in an earlier chapter can be used to arrive at a report format.

As you can see, I'm urging you to use the inverted-pyramid format whenever possible. I think we can do our readers a favor by using such a format.

Still, there are times when this type of format is not necessary or won't work. It's obviously not necessary when no conclusions or recommendations can be reached. In this case, use the straight-line approach. And, the inverted-pyramid approach won't work if, as an example, there are severe limitations to your study. If this is the case, you owe it to your reader to explain the limitations before the conclusions and recommendations are presented.

In short, use a logical format, but keep the reader's needs uppermost in your mind.

SAMPLE REPORTS

Sample report #1: building-block format.   Many of us who have had the building-block format taught to us find it hard to switch to the inverted-pyramid type. The easiest way to make the switch is to first write the report in the building-block pattern and then rearrange the parts into the inverted-pyramid. Often all that is necessary is to move the conclusions and recommendations from the back of the report to the front, right after the introduction.

That was what the writer of this sample report did. The report was written as part of a solution to a management problem. Names of persons and units mentioned in the report have been changed from those involved in the real case.

Here is the report in the building-block format.

To:

From:

Date: September 15, 1979

Subject: Complaints about Service in the Telephone Order Unit

<u>Introduction.</u> At your request I have investigated recent complaints about poor service in the Telephone Order Unit (TOU). The details of the known complaints are these: Two customers complained of excessive waits before their calls were answered, and three customers stated their calls were not answered at all. These five complaints were received between August 11 and September 8. It is reasonable to assume that other customers had similar problems but did not register complaints.

<u>Description of the Telephone Order Unit.</u> The Telephone Order Unit is part of the Customer Service Division (CSD). The function of the TOU is to receive telephone orders over the wide area telephone system and to process all forms, order blanks, and corollary applications related to these orders.

Equipment is standard office equipment and includes a specially designed four-telephone circuit with a rotary answering system. There is a phone on the desk of each employee, but only one bell is used. The bell is mounted on the front wall of the office. When the bell rings, a light on each phone blinks. This system is so designed that when one phone is busy, an incoming call will trigger the bell circuit.

The call can be answered on any of the other phones not in use.

The TOU has four employees—Neumann (the supervisor), Smith, Jones, and Williams.

Results of investigation. A number of circumstances have contributed to the decline of service in the TOU. For one, Neumann, the supervisor, was hospitalized for emergency surgery in mid August, and Jones, who is acting as temporary supervisor, has relegated supervisorial duties to second priority in an attempt to handle the volume of phone calls.

The major problem, however, involves the employee Williams, who transferred into the TOU on August 1. His performance reports in other units have been above average, and his previous supervisors have commented that he is hard working, uncomplaining, and that he does top quality work.

Still, in my visit to the TOU, I noticed that of the employees present Williams answered the fewest phone calls. I asked him why, and he said he just doesn't hear the phone ring. We talked about this some more, and in our conversation Williams admitted he has an irreparable hearing loss. He can hear conversation adequately, face to face or over the telephone, but his ability to hear high frequencies is seriously impaired. Williams admitted he did not mention his hearing problem when he transferred to the TOU for a couple of reasons. For one, he did not think it would interfere with his work. Second, he wanted the job because it meant a raise in pay.

Solutions. Part of the problem will clear up when Neumann returns to work and normal staffing resumes. Otherwise, the solutions involve the following options.

1. Transfer Williams away from duties requiring him to

answer the telephone. We could do this and keep him at his present pay scale. However, we would have the expense of training him at a new position and training someone else to take his place in the TOU.

2. Move the telephone bell from the wall to Williams' desk. Cost, $40 (telephone company service charge). This would help Williams but might place the bell where others cannot hear it.

3. Rearrange the office so Williams sits by the bell. I estimate it would take one hour of staff time to switch work areas. The work involves moving furniture and would alter a seating arrangement that is now apparently liked by all in the TOU. In addition, the only way to avoid disrupting the work routine during the move would be to do it on overtime at an increased salary cost. Also, I think it best to coordinate any such move with the unit's supervisor.

4. Redesign the telephone system so that the bell rings at all four stations. Cost, $40. I consider this the best option.

Conclusions and recommendations. The problem is largely due to a combination of circumstances. One is a specially designed four-line telephone circuit that uses only one bell; the bell cannot be heard by one of the employees who has impaired hearing. In addition, Neumann, the unit's supervisor, has been absent due to illness.

The solution involves either redesigning the telephone system so that the bell will ring at all stations or rearranging the office so that all employees can hear the bell. The first option would require an expenditure of $40 (the telephone company's flat fee service charge) and a minimum disruption of office routine. The second option would disrupt the office routine for approximately one hour and may have a negative impact on morale. In addition, Neumann is not now available, and I think we should coordinate any major rearrangement or reorganization with him.

As you are aware, the average price on each order placed via the TOU is $27,200. Each unanswered call can represent that much lost business. Because of dollar values involved, I recommend we use option one (above) and have the telephone system modified so that it will ring at all four stations. If you would like, I will arrange for the work to be done. I will also explain the situation to Neumann when he returns.

Sample report #2: inverted-pyramid format. Here is the same report in the inverted-pyramid pattern.

To:

From:

Date: September 15, 1979

Subject: Complaints about Service in the Telephone Order Unit

Introduction. At your request I have investigated recent complaints about poor service in the Telephone Order Unit (TOU). The details of the known complaints are these: Two customers complained of excessive waits before their calls were answered, and three customers stated their calls were not answered at all. These five complaints were received between August 11 and September 8. It is reasonable to assume that other customers had similar problems but did not register complaints.

Conclusions and recommendations. The problem is largely due to a combination of circumstances. One is a specially designed four-line telephone circuit that uses only one bell; the bell cannot be heard by one of the employees who has impaired hearing. In addition, Neumann, the unit's supervisor, has been absent due to illness.

The solution involves either redesigning the telephone system so that the bell will ring at all stations or rearranging the office so that all employees can hear the bell. The first option would require an expenditure of $40 (the telephone company's flat fee service charge) and a minimum disruption of office routine. The second option would disrupt the office routine for approximately one hour and may have a negative impact on morale. In addition, Neumann is not now available, and I think we should coordinate any major rearrangement or reorganization with him.

As you are aware, the average price on each order placed via the TOU is $27,200. Each unanswered call can represent that much lost business. Because of dollar values involved, I recommend we use option one and have the telephone system modified so that it will ring at all four stations. If you would like, I will arrange for the work to be done. I will also explain the situation to Neumann when he returns.

For your information I've provided more details on the TOU in the following parts of this memo. The "following parts," not shown here, are the same "Description of the Telephone Order Unit," "Results of Investigation," and "Solutions" that were presented in the example of this report written in building block style.

Sample report #3: an EPRI report.   The following report, written for the Electric Power Research Institute (EPRI), demonstrates many of the features described earlier in this section. The report is reprinted here with explanatory comments provided. Most of the comments point up desirable features, but a few remarks are intended to show areas of possible improvement. Comments in this latter category should not be considered as detracting from the quality of the report, for on the whole it is excellent.

When reading the report, pay particular attention to the format—the arrangement of the abstract, summary and introduction. Although the report does not exactly follow the format recommended earlier, the arrangement used does serve the same purpose: Inform the busy reader as quickly as possible.

COVER FEATURES

1. The cover is orderly and free from distracting clutter.

2. Prominent lettering is used to announce necessary information: title; the EPRI abbreviation (upper right corner) and name spelled out (bottom); report number and date; and name of organization that prepared the report.

3. A special feature of the cover is the set of key words in the upper left corner and just below the title. The key words can be used by readers who have access to computerized information retrieval systems. When key words are typed into such a system, the computer answers back with information on related publications. Depending on the system used, this information could include titles, abstracts, and locations of other reports on the same topic.

EPRI

Power Plant Early Alert Reporting System

Keywords:
  Data Systems
  Alert System
  Power Plant Data

EPRI NP-988
TPS 77-750
Final Report
February 1979

Prepared by
The S. M. Stoller Corporation
Boulder, Colorado

ELECTRIC POWER RESEARCH INSTITUTE

TITLE PAGE FEATURES

1. The title is clearly displayed at the top; all other information is below the title.

2. Names and full addresses of the report's sponsor and the preparing organization are clearly shown.

3. The identifying information also gives the names of the individuals principally involved. Naming these individuals assigns responsibility and credit and gives the reader the name of a person to contact for more information.

Power Plant Early Alert Reporting System

NP-988
Technical Planning Study TPS 77-750

Final Report, February 1979

Prepared by

THE S. M. STOLLER CORPORATION
1919 14th Street
Boulder, Colorado 80302

Principal Investigator
R. H. Koppe

Prepared for

Electric Power Research Institute
3412 Hillview Avenue
Palo Alto, California 94304

EPRI Project Manager
W. L. Lavallee
Nuclear Power Division

COPYRIGHT PAGE FEATURES

1. The ordering information includes the telephone number as an aid to people who wish to speed up the ordering process.

2. The copyright notice is clearly displayed and automatically grants permission to use all or part of the report, provided EPRI is given credit. Many reports are not copyrighted, and most copyright notices do not grant permission; normally, it's necessary to write to the copyright holder and request permission.

3. The notice at the bottom of the page is intended to protect EPRI and the report's authors from legal action that might arise as a result of the report. Different organizations style these legal disclaimers in different ways, and not all organizations see the need for them. The writing of such a notice should be done with the help of an attorney.

ORDERING INFORMATION

Requests for copies of this report should be directed to Research Reports Center (RRC), Box 10090, Palo Alto, CA 94303, (415) 961-9043. There is no charge for reports requested by EPRI member utilities and affiliates, contributing nonmembers, U.S. utility associations, U.S. government agencies (federal, state, and local), media, and foreign organizations with which EPRI has an information exchange agreement. On request, RRC will send a catalog of EPRI reports.

NOTICE

Prepared by
The S. M. Stoller Corporation
Boulder, Colorado

"EPRI PERSPECTIVE" OUTLINE

Paragraph 1. This paragraph presents a key definition (first sentence) and mentions the need for the study (second sentence).

Paragraph 2. This paragraph alerts the reader to additional content.

Paragraphs 3 and 4. The "Conclusions and Recommendations" section begins by offering EPRI's views on implementing recommendations in the report, including the need for further study of points raised in the report.

Paragraph 5. This paragraph cites opposing views concerning one recommendation.

Paragraph 6. Paragraph mentions problems that might be associated with the adoption of another recommendation.

Paragraph 7. This is a summary statement.

The "EPRI Perspective" is an excellent foreword. It establishes the topic, refers to the need for the study, mentions the study's achievements, and points out limitations. These features present EPRI's perspective (view), and the presentation is made in language that is brief and to the point.

EPRI PERSPECTIVE

PROJECT DESCRIPTION
An Early Alert Reporting System (EARS) as presented in this report collects information on significant generic failures in power plants and broadcasts the details of these failures in a timely manner to other utilities, architect-engineers, and manufacturers in an attempt to avert similar failures in other plants. The need for such an alert system was identified in an industry study* of power plant data systems sponsored by the American National Standards Institute (ANSI). As a result of this identified need, the Executive Committee of the Edison Electric Institute's Engineering and Operations Committee requested that EPRI undertake a study to define

the scope and operating methodology for an alert system. This report contains the results of that study.

PROJECT OBJECTIVE
As indicated above, the objective of the project was to define the scope and operating methodology for an alert system. In addition, the manpower requirements and costs were evaluated. The objectives of the project are met in this final report, and the report should provide a sound basis for the further development of an alert system.

CONCLUSIONS AND RECOMMENDATIONS
Although the report makes explicit recommendations on operating an alert system, there are alternatives to the recommendations given, and it will be up to the utility industry and the organization that operates the alert system to make the final decisions on its operation.

Two areas that will probably need further consideration are the reporting of alerts on safety class equipment in nuclear power plants and the timeliness of alert reporting if integrated with a unit outage reporting system.

* Report of the ANSI Steering Committee on Power Plant Data Systems, December, 1977.

The report recommends that safety class equipment not be included in the reporting scope of EARS, because reporting for this equipment is already required by the Nuclear Regulatory Commission (NRC). However, others feel that the NRC reporting does not meet the requirements for an alert system and that safety class equipment should be included in the EARS reporting scope.

The report strongly recommends that EARS be an integral part of an improved outage-cause reporting system. And hence it recommends that unit outage reporting be done monthly in order to accommodate routine alert reporting in a timely manner. (Other reasons for monthly reporting are discussed in the report.) However, the accommodation of alert reporting should not necessarily be the major consideration when deciding how often to report on unit outage. Other things such as the increased reporting burden on the plants must also be considered.

Overall, the report details a workable system informing power plants of potential problems that have significantly affected the performance of other plants.

W. L. Lavallee, Project Manager
Nuclear Power Division

"ABSTRACT" OUTLINE

Paragraph 1.   This paragraph announces the report's scope and purpose.

Paragraph 2.   The second paragraph summarizes the method of gathering data. This paragraph could probably be dropped without altering the usefulness of the abstract.

Paragraph 3.   This paragraph presents a definition necessary to understanding the next paragraph.

Paragraph 4.   This is a statement of a principal conclusion of the report. The conclusion appears again in the "Summary" and in the body of the report. Technically, this conclusion should be called a recommendation, for it recommends a course of action.

Paragraph 5.   Paragraph 5 lists additional content but gives no details on the content.

This abstract is primarily an indicative abstract in that paragraphs 1 and 5 indicate what's in the report proper. The inclusion of paragraphs 3 and 4 give added details, but not enough information is provided so that the abstract can be technically classified as an informative abstract. To be an informative abstract, more specific information would also have to be included in paragraph 5.

ABSTRACT

Technical Planning Study 77-750 was performed for EPRI by The S. M. Stoller Corporation to determine what the scope of an Early Alert Reporting System (EARS) should be, what methodology should be used in implementing and operating it, and what its manpower requirements and cost will be. The purpose of EARS will be to quickly and systematically inform operating power plants of problems which have affected other plants and which might also affect them.

This study was based on work previously done for EPRI (see EPRI reports NP 736 and NP 836) and on interviews with individuals representing utilities, power plant equipment suppliers and government agencies. A total of 52 different organizations were contacted, primarily by phone and/or mail. The results contained in this report were reviewed with many of the people who were originally interviewed and there was near universal agreement that the system described would be useful and should be implemented.

EPRI report NP 836 described two types of data collection which will eventually make up the National Data System which is in early stages of development. One of these two types of data collection is an expanded Outage Cause Reporting System (basically an expansion of the system formerly operated by EEI and recently transferred to NERC).

The principal conclusion of the present report is that EARS should be made part of the Outage Cause Reporting System.

The present report describes the reasons for including EARS in the expanded system. It also describes the implementation and operation of EARS, the role of equipment suppliers in EARS, and expected manpower requirements and costs.

"CONTENTS" FEATURES

The contents list is brief and adequate for a report made up of only 25 pages of double-spaced text. (This figure does not include the front matter of title page, foreword, abstract, content list, and summary.)

Readers would be better served, in a report of any length, if the report's pages were to be numbered consecutively (1, 2, 3, 4, 5, 6, 7, and so on) rather than by section (1-1, 1-2; 2-1, 2-2, 2-3; and so on). The use of consecutive numbering makes it easier to find things.

CONTENTS

"SUMMARY" OUTLINE

Paragraphs 1 and 2. These two paragraphs are almost identical to the first two paragraphs of the report's abstract. Their purpose is to establish the report's scope and purpose (first paragraph) and to describe the method of performing the study (second paragraph).

Paragraph 3. The first sentence summarizes the report's principal conclusion, from the report. Remaining sentences in the paragraph add additional details brought forward from the body of the report.

SUMMARY

Technical Planning Study TPS 77-750 was performed for EPRI by The S. M. Stoller Corporation to determine what the scope of an Early Alert Reporting System (EARS) should be, what methodology should be used in implementing and operating it, and what its manpower requirements and costs will be. The purpose of EARS will be to quickly and systematically inform operating power plants of problems which have affected other plants and which might also affect them.

This study was based on work previously done for EPRI (see EPRI reports NP 736 and NP 836) and on interviews with individuals representing utilities, power plant equipment suppliers and government agencies. A total of 52 different organizations were contacted, primarily by phone and/or mail. The results contained in this report were reviewed with many of the people who were originally interviewed and there was near universal agreement that the system described will be useful and should be implemented.

The principal conclusion of the study is that EARS should be made part of an expanded Outage Cause Reporting System. EPRI report NP 836 described two types of data collection which will eventually make up the National Data System which is now in the early stages of development. One of these two types of data collection is an expanded Outage Cause Reporting System. The expanded Outage Cause Reporting System will basically be an extension of the existing Edison Electric Institute (EEI) Data System. Expansion will consist primarily of more detailed reporting of planned outages, verbal descriptions of outages, and reporting of non-curtailing work on a limited number of major components. Data now reported to the Federal Energy Regulatory Commission (formerly the Federal Power Commission), Nuclear Regulatory Commission (NRC) Gray Books, etc., as well as EEI, will be reported to this single system. Reporting alerts will be a routine part of this data system. The net effect will be to reduce the burden on plant personnel and increase the quality and availability of the data.

| Paragraphs 4, 5, and 6. | These three paragraphs tell how the Early Alert Reporting System (EARS) will work. |
| Paragraph 7. | This paragraph gives three essential pieces of information: system cost, number and types of personnel needed, and how much time is needed to implement the system. |

The "Summary" is well planned and well written. It tells the decision maker (1) what the system is, (2) how it will work, (3) how much it is expected to cost, (4) how many people must be hired to operate it, and (5) how much time is needed to get it started.

The purpose of EARS will be to assist utilities in improving power plant performance. Therefore, it should concentrate on problems which cause plant outages, and combination with the Outage Cause Reporting System is logical. It is often difficult for plant personnel to determine if a problem they have had is of generic significance. If EARS is combined with the Outage Cause Data System, problems deserving of an alert may be identified by the plant, by the data system at the time data is submitted, or in the course of data analysis. Problems deserving an alert are much more likely to be identified in a timely manner by such a system than by a system which requires plants to make special reports of problem alerts.

Once a problem has been identified as a possible alert, the data system will contact the plant by phone and prepare a detailed written description of the problem. If a specific component is involved the alert will be sent to the component vendor. The vendor will have two weeks to comment if desired. Assuming the alert still appears appropriate, it and any vendor comments will be sent to plants with similar equipment. The data system will have a file of engineering data for major components in each plant. When the alert involves a major component or where the component vendor is able to identify plants with similar equipment, the alert will be sent only to plants with that equipment. Where specific plants cannot be identified, it will be necessary to send the alert to all plants. These general alerts will be limited to potentially serious problems.

Alerts sent to any one operating plant will be limited in number and limited to problems likely to affect that plant. Copies of all alerts, as well as analyses of plant performance data and outage cause data will periodically be sent to utility central organizations and will be available to other organizations as requested. EARS will not report problems related to nuclear safety equipment because methods for handling these problems already exist.

An improved Outage Cause Reporting System consisting of both data collection and alerts will cost about $350,000 to develop and $450,000 per year to operate. Operating costs include a staff of five engineers, one technician, and two secretary/clerks. Cost associated with reporting to the system will not be substantially larger than now incurred reporting to existing systems. Development of the Outage Cause System and setting up reporting at five to seven pilot utilities will take about one year. An additional two years will be required to pilot the system, bring remaining utilities into the system, and ultimately supplant existing systems. The complete National Data System will consist of both an improved Outage Cause Reporting System and a detailed Component Reliability Data System. Development of these two systems will be done in parallel but will be largely independent.

By the time readers get to this point, they will have information on which to base actions. The reader wanting still more information will read all or pertinent parts of the remainder of the report.

"INTRODUCTION" OUTLINE

Paragraph 1.   This opening sentence presents a key idea—the failure of power plant equipment. Remaining sentences in the paragraph are used to point out the need for a reporting system and to stress the importance of this need. These sentences also limit the report's scope to a discussion of the need for a system to quickly report generic (characteristic) equipment failures of electrical generating equipment in power plants.

Paragraphs 2   These two paragraphs give background infor-
and 3.   mation on existing reporting systems. In these paragraphs, the authors bolster their argument by referring to the drawbacks of existing systems that take months or years to report outage data.

SECTION 1
INTRODUCTION

The equipment problems faced by an electric power plant range from rather insignificant failures causing little or no loss of production to major component breakdowns resulting in long outages and high attendant costs. Historically, an equipment failure in one particular plant is often the precursor of the same failure in several other plants with similar equipment. If these generic type failures could be recognized by the first one or two plants to experience them, and if the details on these failures could then be broadcast in a timely manner to all other utilities with the same type of equipment, the result would be an opportunity for the forewarned utilities to perform preventative maintenance, make repairs, or perform a design change on the subject equipment during a scheduled shutdown, thus averting an equipment failure and the accompanying forced outage.

There presently exist within the utility industry several avenues for conducting information exchange among plants on the subject of equipment performance. Many equipment failures including numerous low consequence failures are reported by power plants to various industry data bases for the purpose of documenting the effects of the failures on plant productivity, equipment reliability, and/or plant safety. The data collected by these data systems is then summarized in some fashion by the collection agency and fed back to the industry in the form of monthly, quarterly, or yearly reports. The turnaround time on this data ranges from two to three months in the case of nuclear unit outage data reported in the Nuclear Regulatory Commission's "Operating Units Status Report" to one to two years for outage data reported in the Edison Electric Institute's "Report on Equipment Availability for the Ten-Year Period 19xx-19xx."

Another avenue for communication among utilities is the Edison Electric Institute's committee meeting and information exchange structure. The EEI Prime Movers Committee meets three times a year and conducts a "round table" discussion of power plant operating experience during these meetings. An "Operating Experience Report" is compiled from the round table discussions for use by members of the Prime Movers Committee. EEI also sponsors a Nuclear Plant Information Exchange Program which collects information from participating plants principally in the form of Licensee Event Reports and compiles the information into a single volume for distribution to the participating plants. A number of equipment suppliers provide problem bulletins, and some provide information on such things as recent operating experience and estimated repair times.

Paragraph 4.   This paragraph points to deficiencies in existing systems. The last sentence of this paragraph brings in the subject of the report. Some readers would probably like a more pronounced statement of the subject, other than burying it at the bottom of a long paragraph in the middle of a page. In defense of this technique, it must be pointed out that the subject has appeared so far on the cover and title page and in the "EPRI Perspective," "Abstract," and "Summary."

Paragraph 5. This paragraph announces the purpose of the study.

Paragraphs 6 and 7. These paragraphs discuss the method of conducting the study. Note that 48 "interviews were conducted" (paragraph 6), but 52 "organizations were contacted" ("Abstract" and "Summary"). Presumably, some of the organizations contacted did not grant interviews, a point that should have been clarified.

All forms of information exchange mentioned here provide a necessary service to the utility industry, but all are limited in their ability to provide an early alert of impending generic plant equipment problems. None of the existing methods of information exchange has a short enough information turn-around time nor the singular purpose of providing an effective early alert system. For example, in trying to obtain indicators of impending equipment problems from existing industry data bases, a utility is faced not only with the information lag time but also with a large quantity of data from which information must be extracted pertaining to its particular equipment. The task of extracting useful information can be quite formidable. The purpose of EARS will be to quickly and systematically inform plants with a particular component or system when a problem arises with a similar item in another plant.

The purpose of this Technical Planning Study was to determine what the scope of EARS should be, what methodology should be used in implementing and operating it, and what its manpower requirements and costs will be.

During the course of this study interviews were conducted with 9 organizations manufacturing turbines or boilers, 19 organizations manufacturing other power plant equipment, and 20 utilities. Most interviews were conducted by mail and telephone, although a few involved face-to-face contact.

Much of the work involved in the study consisted of developing a consensus among a considerable number of persons, many with differing viewpoints. The EAR System described in this report will not satisfy everyone on every point. However, we believe that it will serve a useful function and that it will satisfy the needs of most organizations within the utility industry.

Paragraph 8. This paragraph previews the rest of the report.

Certainly the most important conclusion of this work is that an Early Alert System should be a part of an improved Outage Cause Reporting System. The need for such a system was identified in a previous EPRI Study (see EPRI NP-836). Section 2 of this report briefly describes the system and presents the rationale for including EARS within it. Another EPRI project to define in detail the data to be collected is now underway. Section 3 of this report describes the way alerts should be handled within the Outage Cause System, and Section 4 describes other uses of outage cause data which, while not specifically alerts, serve a complementary function. Section 5 describes the way in which the Outage Cause/Alert System will interface with existing systems. Finally, Section 6 describes the methods, costs and schedule for implementation of EARS.

The remainder of the report contains support material.

II-D.

PROPOSALS

A proposal is a sales tool, a written offer to perform a service or to manufacture a product for money. Proposals are used in industry, education, and government for the purpose of securing contracts or grants from government or private sources. Any number of types of sales are made with proposals. Major weapons systems are sold to the Department of Defense via proposals. Individual components are subcontracted through proposals. Food service programs are sold by proposals. Research grants are won with proposals. The idea for this book was sold with a proposal.

In short, proposals are a basic part of the way we do business, and a successful proposal can mean money for you or your organization. Because of the value attached to proposals, it will be beneficial to take a look here at the important aspects of proposal writing, beginning with a discussion of a proposal's special characteristics.

SPECIAL CHARACTERISTICS OF PROPOSALS

First, proposals are classified in two ways: *solicited* and *unsolicited*.

A solicited proposal is written in response to a formal request, frequently called a request for proposal (RFP). A solicited proposal offers something that the customer has expressed a need for. More than likely the customer has described the need in considerable detail. In addition, the customer has said that money is available for the project. Nevertheless, other firms are competing for the same contract, so the solicited proposal must be designed to convince the customer that your company's offering is the right one.

An unsolicited proposal offers something that the customer has not asked for, may not be familiar with, and may not have the money for. Accordingly, the unsolicited proposal should be planned to indicate the need for the product or service. Indicating need may not be enough; you may also have to influence the customer's desire. Furthermore, you might even have to go so far as to suggest a method of funding. An unsolicited proposal may be just as worthwhile as a solicited one; the two are just written under different conditions.

A second characteristic of proposals concerns the method of preparation. Typically, a proposal is prepared under a tight deadline and is the product of a team effort. The team can include representatives from administration, sales, technical, cost estimating, legal, and graphic arts departments. In addition, a writer or editor should be assigned to the team to resolve matters of format, punctuation, style, and grammar.

Third, and perhaps most important, is that a proposal is not only read, it is *evaluated*. Evaluators look closely at your company's approach, resources, and qualifications. And everything in the proposal is evaluated. This includes the accuracy and consistency with which the proposal was written and edited. In other words, it's a lot like having a term paper graded, only the outcome can be a lot better or a lot worse.

FORMAT OF A PROPOSAL

Sometimes the RFP will specify a format that must be adhered to. When a format is not specified, it is best to arrange the proposal to accomplish three major tasks, in this order: First, show that a need exists for a product or service. Second, show how your organization will satisfy that need. Third, show why your organization is qualified to perform the service or manufacture the product; in other words, show why your organization should get the money.

Many proposal writers in technical and scientific fields use a fairly standardized format that follows the general arrangement suggested above. This format also lends itself to nontechnical subjects. The parts of the format are usually labeled Introduction, Technical Plan, Management Plan, and Capabilities. Costs are sometimes itemized toward the end of the proposal. Other sections as well as appendixes may be added. The content of these various sections is covered here. During your reading of the following discussion, you may find it helpful to refer to the two sample proposals included at the end of the section.

Front matter.   The title page (1) tells the reader that the document is a proposal, (2) displays the title, and (3) gives the project number, if one has been assigned:

PROPOSAL TO PROVIDE BUSINESS
AVIATION MAINTENANCE SERVICES AT
HOLLYWOOD-BURBANK AIRPORT
RFP PROJECT 81-3-251

An abstract or summary or both may be used, followed by a contents list. These are written in the same manner as for a report.

Introduction.   Lead off with a summary of the problem that the proposal seeks to solve. If the proposal is being written in response to a request for proposal, don't simply restate the language of the RFP; the evaluators already know that. Expand on that language and show that (1) you understand the basic requirements and (2) you are aware of any probable difficulties that may arise.

Then, in concise terms, offer the solution. It is important at this point, and whenever possible throughout the proposal, to stress customer benefits. You can do this by pointing out what is unique or special about your solution, or you can describe how your method is an improvement over other methods. If possible, stress customer benefits in terms of dollars, numbers, or percentages. Can you—

1. Predict a success rate? Has your system proved 95 percent effective compared to competitors' 90 percent, 88 percent, 82 percent, or other values?

2. Establish cost effectiveness? Will your system do the job at 7 cents per unit, while the other systems cost 9 cents, 11 cents, or more per unit?

3. Talk in terms of profits? Have previous users of your product or system reported gains? Of how much—30 percent, 40 percent?

In other words, your solution must stress how it will solve the problem efficiently, effectively, and productively.

In addition, introductory material should include a preview of the body of the proposal. The preview should focus attention on the important parts and should not be merely a rehash of the table of contents.

Technical plan (work statement). The technical plan describes in detail the work you are going to do as your part of the bargain. Here you should identify specific tasks in concrete and definite language. Provide detailed descriptions, and use visual aids to supplement the descriptions. Organize the description in the order in which tasks will be accomplished. If your solution is new or unique, explain it thoroughly. And if you have rejected any solutions, mention them and give the reasons for rejection.

Other appropriate topics here are research techniques, including requirements for test specimens, laboratory animals, or subjects; unique system hardware; design, performance, or engineering specifications; testing and evaluation procedures; a data management plan that specifies the type of data to be collected, methods of handling, processing, reduction, and evaluating; schedules or flow diagrams; and description of facilities and equipment, both available and to be purchased.

Management plan. The management portion of the proposal tells how you're going to manage the contract after you get it. Here you have to convince the client that your company's management philosophy is sound and reliable.

An organization chart should be inserted here. If the entire organization is not working on the project, the chart should be marked to indicate which units are. Personnel working on the project should be identified and their assignments given. You should also show whether a special group will be formed to manage the project or how the project is to be integrated into the organization's regular structure.

Other topics include schedules, timetables, and milestones; accounting practices; reporting procedures and documentation processes; quality assurance and quality control methods; financial resources; company size and history; agreements with unions; collective bargaining history; personnel manpower controls; and management objectives.

The management plan section can also contain a description of the method used to manage past similar projects.

Capabilities. Common to almost every proposal is a section on the experience and capabilities of your company. Besides company history, this section contains resumés of key personnel assigned to the project. Data on the company's performance can be drawn from annual reports, past proposals, newspaper clippings, and press releases. Achieved performance on past projects can be compared to requirements. To save preparation time, much of this material, including the resumés, should be written in draft form and kept on file. Then, when the proposal is being written, the capabilities section can be slanted to the project mentioned in the proposal.

Costs. Often a request for proposal will specify that costs be put into a separate volume apart from the main body of the proposal. The theory is that the technical evaluation should be made without regard to cost. Regardless of where the cost section is put, it is a detailed and complete listing of all costs. It shows unit prices for everything—hours to be worked, space, facilities, components. And it should, as much as possible, project cost changes due to inflation or other anticipated economic influences.

Other sections. Sometimes a conclusions section is added at the end to reemphasize important points. Appendixes of lengthy mathematical calculations or support material not necessary to the basic text can be added.

INTEGRATING THE SALES APPROACH

The language of a proposal is that of the soft-sell. Its success depends on an unemotional, thorough, and positive approach. Some steps to help develop that approach are listed here.

1. Know your product. Your product is a service or a manufactured item. What is it like in total? What is it like in its specifics? How is it better than any other similar service or item? What are its strong points? Where are its weaknesses? Answer these questions for yourself. Then write the proposal to show that you know your product thoroughly.

2. Know your market. First, know your competition. What are they good at? Where are their weaknesses? How big is the competition? Write the proposal to show how you can do the project better than the competition.

Next, if you have questions about the RFP, or if you are writing an unsolicited proposal, query the funder. A seasoned writer queries an editor to find out what's expected in a manuscript; a proposal writer should query the funder. Try to find the key person who can tell you what's "in." Try to find out who's on the evaluation committee and what the committee is looking for. Don't be afraid to ask for advice. Obtain all the information you can on the plans, desires, likes, dislikes, and prejudices of the buyer. "Never assume anything. If there is the least doubt as to what the customer wants, ask him before proceeding further."[4]

3. Attract attention. Your job here is to write a strong introduction and to keep the introduction related to the topic. Orient the introductory material to the nontechnical reader. The nontechnical reader will probably read no more than the introduction, and "In many cases the nontechnical reader may be the most influential reader."[5]

Also, a proposal should look professional but not flashy. Many proposals are typed, double-spaced, on 8½ x 11 paper. When preparing a proposal:

- •Do — Pick a binder that will allow easy removal of the pages. A proposal is sometimes taken apart to be reviewed by several people simultaneously.
- •Do — Proofread thoroughly. A professional presentation is free of misspelled words and typographical errors.
- •Don't — Use binders that are decorated with loud colors or wild patterns. These have negative psychological effects on many people.
- •Don't — Use excessive underlining or quotation marks in the text. The overuse of these devices clutters the page and diverts attention from the content of the writing.

4. Arouse interest and desire. Advertising specialists would tell us to appeal to the reader's logic, emotions, or both. That would be good advice if you were selling shampoo or deodorant. But a proposal is examined by a team of hard-nosed evaluators. Emotional appeals won't work, and you'll have to develop a logical appeal. A logical appeal is based on *showing*—with numbers and cold, hard facts—how your proposal will benefit the buyer.

Here's an example of the factual detail that helps make the sale. The example is from a proposal by the Federal Express' Technical Publications Section in Memphis, Tennessee.

The proposed text management system consists of an [equipment identification] with a lease cost of $475 per month. The system is a specialized text management device, keyboard controlled, with a video display terminal.

Output is photographic quality black on white type in various fonts in sizes from 6 to 72 points. . . .

Current methods of producing text require that when a page is retyped due to change the entire page must be edited. Pages retyped using the proposed system require that only the changed portion of the page be edited. Therefore a savings of at least 50 percent is achieved. Fifty percent saving of the current editing time of 4 hours per day (by the writers and typist) would result in a monthly savings of $200/Mo based on an $800 typist salary and $300/Mo based on a $1200 writer's salary for a total of $500/Mo. . . .

The current annual publications printing expenses are $29,633. Considering the attached sample sheets of the proposed printing method and the currently used printing method, it can easily be seen that a substantial printing savings is involved. Three and one-half sheets of type are condensed onto one sheet. Providing that one-half of the printing expense is related to forms, single-sheet changes or purchase of type, the 1:3.5 savings would be effective on $14,816. (.5 x $29,633 Annual Printing Expense).

Printing savings then are ⅔ x $14,816 = $9,779/Yr savings or $815/Mo.

5. *Convince judgment.* To convince judgment—

- Place the strongest material first. Unimpressive material placed first causes the reader to lose interest. Weak material placed first causes the reader to look for weaknesses in the material that follows.
- Write the proposal so that it cannot be misunderstood. Give the details. Use specific, concrete language. Don't write about *optimum;* instead, give numbers and percentages.
- Be honest. Leave out the fancy rhetoric. Make clear what is mandatory and what is not. If a contract results, you have to uphold your end of the bargain.
- Show self-confidence and enthusiasm. Write about what *shall* and *will* be done over what *should* and *would* be done.
- Establish a consistent editorial style. Consistency builds reader confidence. Headings, capitalization, punctuation, and use of numbers should be standard throughout the proposal.

6. *Stimulate to action.* The entire proposal is aimed at securing action. No coupon to clip at the end can possibly overcome

an imprecise technical section, a fuzzy management plan, or a lack of capabilities. However, you can spur the proposal's evaluation a little bit if you

- Set up key action steps as headings
- Impart a sense of urgency by listing key dates
- Make it easy to find who's in charge by placing the project manager's name and telephone number on the cover and on the title page

PITFALLS

"It is not generally realized how many proposals are rejected early in the evaluation process just because the bidder did not read or understand the RFP. Almost fifty percent of all proposals received are declared non-responsive for the simple reason that the bidder did not grasp the problem or did not respond to the requirements or attempted to sell a product which was (beyond reason) more than what the customer asked."[6]

To avoid this pitfall, you have to ensure that every requirement stated in the RFP has been satisfied. Study the RFP with care. Have everyone on the proposal preparation team read the RFP. Systematically check from the RFP to the proposal draft. Notify the proposal manager of any omissions.

Other major reasons for rejection, other than costs, are "oversimplification, . . . overoptimism," and "vague generalities and sweeping statements which appear to cover a lack of knowledge."[7]

In short, know exactly what it is you're about and use the right language.

SAMPLE PROPOSALS

Two sample proposals are included. The first is on a subject in the physical sciences; the second concerns a subject in the social sciences. Both proposals have been edited to alter factual material such as names, locations, budgets, and any other data that might compromise the business approach and competitive style of the organization preparing the proposal. In addition, the first sample is shown in condensed form, for in its original version, it was as long as this book. What has been retained, however, is the spirit and structure of each proposal. Each will be useful as a source of ideas.

Sample proposal #1. This first sample proposal was written in response to a request for proposal (RFP). The organization of the proposal closely follows the format used by many proposal writers in scientific and technical fields. That is, it presents, in order, the Introduction, Technical Plan, and Management Plan. When reading the proposal, pay particular attention to the Introduction. It presents the key topics of problem definition, the method proposed to deal with the problem, the benefits of the proposed method, and the company's capabilities. The language of the Introduction has been simplified to reach as many nontechnical readers are possible, and headings are used to attract attention to main ideas.

A PROPOSAL
TO
RELOCATE
CHANNEL 4's
ANTENNA
RFP 79–365

SECTION 1.0

INTRODUCTION

1.1   PROBLEM DEFINITION

Channel 4's antenna was erected when the station went on the air over 25 years ago. Since then, Channel 4's viewing area has increased in population, and the center of population has shifted approximately 14 miles to the south. As a result of these population changes, approximately 200,000 people live immediately outside Channel 4's prime viewing area. If Channel 4's antenna could be relocated to serve the television station's present audience and potential audience, it is estimated that audience size would increase by at least nine percent. An additional gain might be realized if the height of the antenna support tower could be increased.

1.2   PROGRAM OBJECTIVES

To relocate Channel 4's antenna to the best possible site, Argus proposes a program with these two objectives:

1. Conduct a thorough survey of available high-terrain sites
2. Establish signal strengths in core and fringe areas.

1.3   APPROACH

Our antenna relocation program will be conducted in three phases: Phase 1, Preliminary Investigation, Field Survey, and Test Planning; Phase 2, Site Selection and Field Testing; Phase 3, Final Testing and Final Report. Total program length will be 10 months.

1.3.1   Phase 1 (two months)

Phase 1 involves determining high terrain features and developing test methods. High terrain features will be established by using U. S. Geological Survey Maps, Aeronautical Charts, and aerial survey. Test methods will involve the calibration of meters to accurately measure signal strength prior to subjective viewer analysis. At the end of Phase 1, an informal letter report will be prepared by Argus and reviewed by Channel 4 prior to starting Phase 2.

1.3.2 Phase 2 (four months)

During Phase 2, Argus will provide complete data on at least three possible sites that are available for purchase or lease by Channel 4. Data will include the geographic location of each site and predicted viewing areas for different antenna heights at each site. Selection of the final site will be made by Channel 4, in consultation with Argus. When the site has been selected and the land acquired by Channel 4, Argus will erect the tower and install the antenna.

1.3.3 Phase 3 (four months)

Phase 3 is the testing and acceptance period. During the first phase of testing, a vertical color bar video pattern and a 4,000 Hertz audio signal will be transmitted continually at normal station power during night scheduled off-the-air periods. This phase of testing will last three months. Signal strength will be measured with Barth meters, and the color-bar test pattern will be observed in the fringe diameter to subjectively evaluate definition. This phase will also consist of necessary safety inspections and certification of tower guy wires, electrical terminals and wiring, and lighting. The final month of Phase 3 will be given over to viewer evaluation of reception from the new antenna; this evaulation will be done by questionnaire.

1.4 BENEFITS

Three benefits will result:

1. Channel 4 will have the most complete listing of potential and available sites from which to choose a new location for its antenna.

2. Thorough testing and reception measurement in the viewing area will be conducted before and after antenna erection; this testing will ensure the best possi-

ble site selection and provide Channel 4 complete data on which to base acceptance.

3. The final report will be planned and written for maximum use by Channel 4's advertising sales department.

1.5 ARGUS CAPABILITIES

Since 1951, Argus has been active in VHF and UHF circuit and antenna design. We have worked with Channel 4 on the station's previous antenna, and we have served as consultants to other television stations for their antenna siting. As consultants to the Federal Communications Commission (FCC) we have just completed a nationwide study of VHF viewing areas.

To conduct that study, Argus contracted with a consultant, Edward Morton. Mr. Morton was formerly a chief engineer with RCA. Feeling that Mr. Morton would be uniquely qualified to help us with Channel 4's antenna relocation, Argus has engaged him for this effort. Mr. Morton will personally review the approximately 11 potential sites and recommend 3 from which final selection will be made by Channel 4. Mr. Morton will assist Argus engineers in conducting site surveys and in designing the tower and antenna.

The program director will be Arthur Dillingham, who was program director for the erection of Channel 9's new antenna. The principal engineer will be Willis Conway, who is now doing similar work for Channel 6 at Springfield. Assisting Mr. Conway will be personnel with previous experience on related programs: James McGhee, test director; Robert Mackey, manager of structure engineering; and Megan Anderson, data analyst and programmer. Mr. McGhee and Mr. Mackey have both had extensive experience in their fields, and Ms. Anderson is nationally known for her work with computer processed data on radiation patterns.

Overall, Argus offers Channel 4 a staff with the most expertise and one that will relocate the antenna with maximum cost effectiveness.

SECTION 2.0

TECHNICAL PLAN

The proposed antenna relocation will be conducted in three phases. Figure II-D1 presents an overview of the program.

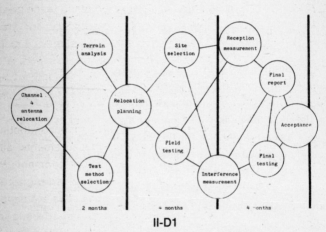

II-D1

Phase 1 will involve two months of investigation and planning. Terrain and line-of-sight data from possible locations will be analyzed, and the various sites will be assigned to similarity groups. A representative site from each group will then be selected for the Phase 2 study. At the same time, data from Argus' files and from the literature will be analyzed to assess the accuracy and validity of existing radiation factors and to determine where additional test information is required. In addition, the test methods to be used in Phase 2 will be selected and checked during Phase

1. The product of Phase 1 will be a survey and test plan for the sites to be surveyed and the test methodology to be used.

Phase 2 will begin four months of field survey and testing. The primary objective of the field survey will be to determine the location of the best possible site and to establish design parameters for the antenna and support tower. In conjunction with on-site surveys, we plan to conduct informal testing of reception by using a mobile VHF antenna and measuring signal strength at selected points for each possible antenna site within Channel 4's potential viewing area. Also during Phase 2 we plan to conduct tests on wind resistance and stability of various antenna support towers. The most visible outcomes of Phase 2 will be erection of the tower and installation of the antenna at a site to be selected by Channel 4.

The last four months (Phase 3) will be spent in conducting interference measurements, reception measurements, and final testing. Interference and reception measurements involve the accurate measurement of signal strengths in fringe and core viewing areas and the subjective evaluation of video and audio quality in these areas. Final testing involves one month of viewer evaluation in selected households in what were formerly fringe areas.

The last step in the program will be the preparation of a final report that will consist of two major sections. The first major section will show how much Channel 4's viewing area has expanded as a result of antenna relocation. Data will be presented in terms of increased geographical coverage (hundreds of square miles) and increased number of potential viewers; this last set of data will be broken down into urban, suburban, rural, and industrial listings. The second major section of the final report will contain the details of terrain and line-of-sight analyses, field testing, reception and interference measurements, and final testing.

Details of various elements of the program are presented in the sections that follow.

2.1   TERRAIN AND LINE-OF-SIGHT ANALYSIS

The first step in the antenna relocation program involves determining high terrain features and line-of-sight radiation patterns. . . .

The next step is to establish if any uncharted man-made structures that now exist or that are planned would block Channel 4's signal. . . .

2.2   SITE SELECTION

It appears at present that 11 potential antenna sites exist and are available for lease or purchase by Channel 4. These sites are all points of high terrain that can be used to provide television coverage to Channel 4's existing audience while extending service to a larger audience. The 11 sites are located in a west-south-east arc that has its center 18 miles south of the present antenna. The nature of the terrain on that arc is such that the 11 sites are distributed in three clusters.

2.3   FIELD TESTING

Site selection calculations will be backed up by informal field testing. This testing will consist of moving a mobile VHF transmitter to each of the three representative sites and transmitting test audio and video at night while Channel 4 is off the air. Signal measurements will be used to confirm the Hennelly Grid suppositions for the height of the mobile antenna, which is 50 feet when fully raised. By extension, these measurements can be used to confirm Hennelly Grid suppositions for other antenna heights. A particular concern of informal testing is the establishment of a site or sites from which reception will be free of ghosts.

Formal field testing will begin as soon as the permanent antenna has been placed on its tower. During the first phase of formal field testing a vertical color-bar video pattern and a 4,000 Hertz audio signal will be transmitted continually at normal station power during night scheduled off-the-air periods. This first phase of formal field testing will last three months. During this phase, signal strengths will be measured with Barth meters in core and fringe areas. In addition, the color-bar test pattern will be observed in the fringe diameter to subjectively evaluate definition. This first phase will also include safety inspections and certification of tower guy wires, electrical terminals and wiring, and lighting. . . .

SECTION 3.0

MANAGEMENT PLAN

3.1 PROGRAM ORGANIZATION AND PERSONNEL

The Channel 4 Antenna Relocation Program will be managed out of Argus' home office under the direction of Arthur Dillingham, Manager of VHF Design Programs. Mr. Dillingham will have the total responsibility for fulfilling the contract requirements on schedule and within the budget. He will be the point of contact for Channel 4's staff. Mr. Dillingham reports to James Gobel, Manager of the Antenna Design Division, who in turn reports to Wayne Johnson, Argus' general manager. (Argus is organized as shown in Figure II-D2.) Mr. Johnson has had extensive experience in both UHF and VHF antenna design and installation, having been the program manager for the VIDSAT program of the National Aeronautics and Space Administration.

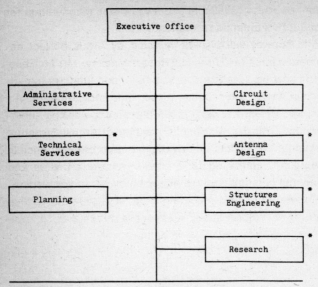

* Units primarily responsible for project

II-D2

Willis Conway will be the principal engineer for the program and will be responsible to Mr. Dillingham for the day-to-day operations of the program. Mr. Conway is currently performing in a similar role for Channel 6 at Springfield; his effort on that program should be completed about the same time that Channel 4's antenna relocation program is initiated. Assisting Mr. Conway as principal consultant will be Edward Morton, a consulting electronics engineer with over 20 years of experience. Eighteen of those years were spent in VHF and UHF antenna design; the last two years he served as a chief engineer with RCA. Mr. Morton is a favorite consultant for the Federal Communications Commission (FCC). In the past three years he has conducted several studies for the FCC involving the analysis of radiation patterns of tall-tower antennas. Mr. Morton is by far the most qualified person available to act as principal consultant for Channel 4's antenna relocation.

Mr. Conway will also be assisted by Argus project engineers James McGhee and Robert Mackey. Mr. McGhee, who is Argus' test director, has also had extensive experience in antenna design and placement. Prior to joining Argus, Mr. McGhee served as VHF circuit engineering supervisor for CBS. Mr. Mackey is manager of Argus' Structure Engineering Division. He has over 15 years of experience in designing, fabricating, and erecting antenna towers and constructing and installing antenna power transfer systems. Both Mr. McGhee and Mr. Mackey were full-time participants in the installation of Channel 3's antenna on Mt. Walnut.

Megan Anderson will be the principal data analyst on this program. Ms. Anderson is one of the most experienced people in the business in the preparation of computer processed data on radiation patterns. She is currently conducting a study of weather-related skip-reception patterns for the FCC.

3.2 PROGRESS REVIEW

Argus plans to maintain total coordination with Channel 4's Engineering Division. At the end of the first month of the program, we will meet with key members of Channel 4's staff and establish points of contact for the day-to-day exchange of information. The next technical review meeting will be held at the end of the second month when the Phase 1 planning is largely completed. At this time, we will go over the detailed plans for Phase 2. From then on, twice-monthly coordination meetings will be held. In addition to the twice-monthly meetings with Channel 4, Argus will conduct an in-house monthly program review. At this in-house meeting, which will coincide with the preparation of the monthly progress report to Channel 4, the principal engineer will review the program status with the program director and the Argus general manager. Channel 4 personnel are welcome at Argus' monthly program review meetings.

3.3 DOCUMENTATION

3.3.1 Monthly Progress Reports

Argus will keep Channel 4's Engineering Division manager informed on the progress of the program through informal monthly letter progress reports. These reports will assess progress by task against the program schedule and the funds expended. These letter-reports will also cite the problems encountered that might necessitate or make desirable changes in the program. Any changes will be negotiated in advance.

3.3.2 Final Report

This report will be submitted in draft form (10 copies) to Channel 4 at the end of 10 months. The report will consist of two major sections. The first major section will show how much Channel 4's viewing area has expanded as a result of antenna relocation. Data will be presented in terms of increased geographical coverage (hundreds of square miles) and increased number of potential viewers. This last set of data will be broken down into lists of new communities and industries served. Increased viewing coverage will be identified as urban, suburban, and rural; these groups will be keyed with market identification numbers from the Television Industry Market Quarterly. The second major section of the report will contain the details of terrain and line-of-sight analyses, field testing, reception and interference measurements, and final testing. . . .

3.4 QUALITY CONTROL

The quality control portion of this program will consist of

Phase 1 testing to develop methodology and establish accuracy and precision for using the Barth meters, plus the normal calibration and redundant measuring that are routine parts of Argus' field testing.

3.4.1   Phase 1

Argus has used the Barth meters in the field for preliminary tests with satisfactory results. We have observed good agreement between the Barth meters and other test methods. However, no attempt has been made to establish and record the accuracy and precision associated with the meters. We plan to do this during Phase 1. . . .

3.4.2   Phase 2 and Phase 3

During Phase 2 and Phase 3, Barth meters will be used to measure signal strength in core and fringe areas. The primary quality control technique during these phases will be to maintain a supply of three Barth meters. At the beginning of each test day, redundant measurements will be made of each parameter, using different Barth meters. If two meters agree, testing will proceed, using one of the two meters that agree. If two meters disagree, the difference will be resolved by using the third meter. Sufficient laboratory testing will be performed to determine if the disagreeing meter is defective or needs calibration. Anytime that an unusual reading, either too high or too low, is experienced, additional tests will be run. The test engineers' notebooks will contain complete details of all individual test procedures.

Argus has a routine quality control program that involves periodic calibration of all of our instruments, meters, and. . . .

Sample proposal #2.[8]   In this proposal, the headings used are different from the headings used in sample proposal #1. Still, the organizational pattern is generally the same: Establish the problem, describe the method planned to deal with the problem, and cite capabilities.

Proposal for

A STUDY OF
POLICE-COMMUNITY RELATIONS
PRACTICES

Submitted by:

Center on Urban Problems
1000 A Street, N.W.
Washington, D.C. 20001

For further information, contact:

Charles Brown
Executive Director
202/123-4567

PROPOSAL FOR
A STUDY OF POLICE-COMMUNITY
RELATIONS PRACTICES

PURPOSE:

The purposes of the proposed study are as follows:

1. to study police-community relations practices in a number of American cities where the problem of police-community relations is of major significance
2. to evaluate the effectiveness of practices and programs, and to report on those which are effective or harmful
3. to publish a preliminary report four to five months after the study is funded
4. to disseminate a preliminary report and encourage discussion through national or regional conferences and by local police force officials and community committees
5. to publish a final report and encourage implementation of promising practices
6. to encourage additional research

The relationship between America's minority groups—black, Puerto Rican, and Chicano—and the police seems to have reached a critical stage. Such factors as a rapid increase in population, increased proportion of young people in that population, migration from rural to urban areas, and increasing complexity of urban life and protest against discrimination have all contributed to the problems of law enforcement. These problems, although not created by police behavior, have nevertheless resulted in behavior which has created problems for the police. The nature of police response has frequently alienated transgressors as well as law-abiding citizens.

Recent studies published by the President's Commission on Law Enforcement and other institutions have revealed that blacks are eager for more police protection but feel that they are less likely to be treated fairly by police.

There is much evidence to indicate tension between municipal and state police forces and members of minority communities. Although much of what is occurring results from vast social dislocations and general attitudes of prejudice and contempt, many police departments have recognized the necessity for improving the relationship between law enforcement agents and minority community members. Although such efforts obviously fall short of solving basic societal problems, they nevertheless seek to establish communication links between police and minorities, to seek cooperation from minority organizations, and to convince the minority community of the justice of police behavior.

Police-Community Relations Practices

One of the most promising new programs seeking to improve these strained relationships has been the development of police-community relations bureaus. Within these bureaus a variety of techniques is used, some with apparent effectiveness.

In the past few years we have seen the number of such bureaus multiply. The very rapidity with which such programs have been adopted has created some doubt regarding their eventual efficacy. Reports from some communities suggest that such bureaus have been, at least, moderately successful. Others have claimed a high degree of effectiveness. William E. Miller, assistant and legal adviser to retired Superintendent Walker Oliver of the St. Louis, Mo., Police Department, has claimed that a program of police-community workshops has helped to prevent a major riot in that city.

Given our present knowledge, it is difficult to evaluate the claims offered by police-community relations bureaus. Many police departments appear to be "latching on" to a new fad without making a genuine effort to understand the intrinsic nature of a police-community relations program. For some it appears to be a public relations device intended to "sell" the police department to the minority community without the concomitant need to be ready to work with that community.

In some cases, it appears that the creation of a police-community relations bureau has been instituted without the reform of police authorities, in spite of the high-sounding "Statement of Purposes" proclaimed in establishing the bureau.

Some police practices seem to affect police-community relations positively. We intend to study existing police-community relations practices in order to:

(1) develop evaluative tools which will permit us to determine the success of bureaus and various techniques in improving police-community relations

(2) determine the scope and function of community relations techniques

(3) analyze the organization, forms of supervision, and responsibility of community relations bureaus

(4) analyze the recruitment, qualifications, and training of personnel involved in community relations practices

(5) examine the opinions of police administration, patrolmen, minority group leaders, and others with regard to community relations practices.

The study will seek to identify and describe promising practices as well as deleterious performances so that:

(1) departments can improve the quality of police work as it relates to minority groups

(2) necessary changes in organization and police behavior can be encouraged

(3) training of squad members and all other police can be improved

(4) additional communities will be encouraged to establish effective bureaus and initiate improved community relations practices.

<u>Method:</u>

1. A team of social scientists, research-writers, law enforcement experts, and CUP staff will examine police-community relations views and practices in a selected number of cities. Since CUP staff has had extensive contact with police work throughout the country, there will be little delay in pinpointing the cities in which highly effective or undesirable practices are employed.

2. The project staff and CUP personnel will first meet to define the study and develop a standard methodology to be followed. For example, the practices to be studied might be analyzed in relation to the following criteria:

support by minority group members
effectiveness
responsibility
relation to police administration
relation to precincts
support of the department
authority as to jurisdiction
citizen contact
policy formulation
personnel decisions
training
handling of high tension situations
evaluation and relevant research.

3. Project personnel will interview police, minority group representatives, civic officials, media representatives, and other appropriate people in the communities concerned.

4. A detailed examination will be undertaken of available research which would be related to investigation in any community. Thus in Watts, Detroit, or Newark, where research on riots has been completed or is in progress, findings will be disseminated and the community will be examined, and its relationship to the study evaluated.

5. Among the practices to be examined will be community relations bureaus, neighborhood meetings, using minority youth as police auxiliaries, storefront neighborhood offices, human relations training for police, ombudsman techniques, etc.

6. Project personnel will meet as frequently as possible (preferably semi-monthly) for evaluation meetings and progress reports.

7. It is likely that a preliminary report, which will be valuable for guidance of police departments, will be available from four to five months after the project is approved.

8. The process of applying the report's findings can be summarized as follows:

a. distribution of preliminary report to appropriate police and civic officials

b. local and regional meetings of police and civic officials

c. meetings with local minority community leadership

d. eventual national conference (separately funded) involving police authorities, community leadership, and academic police experts

9. The posture of the report will be to publicize those practices which maintain good police-community relations, and to identify the cities utilizing those practices. Cities

whose practices are not effective or harmful will not be identified. The reason for this is our desire to use good community relations practices ourselves in an effort to encourage police to take action. We do not want to arouse antagonism and controversy by specific accusations. We are determined to use every means at our disposal to improve community relations practices. We plan to do this not only through publication of our findings but by any other means available to us. These include conferences with organizations such as local Police Chiefs' Associations, Police Benevolent Associations, and state and community organizations.

Conduct of the Study

While the study will be under the general supervision of Charles Brown, CUP's executive director, major responsibility will rest with Mr. Lloyd Solomon, assistant program director. (A replacement for Mr. Solomon during the period of the study will be hired.)

The study of police-community relations practices can be performed effectively by an objective non-police-linked organization such as the Center on Urban Problems.

The Center has had considerable experience in working with both police groups and academic research organizations. We have been involved in recent years in a major study with the Center for Urban Research at Bleeker University, San Francisco, Calif. The Center has been involved in a number of projects and publications with the International Association of Chiefs of Police, the Southern Police Institute, and a variety of state and municipal police organizations. In addition, the Center, by virtue of intense community contacts developed through a system of 28 regional offices scattered across the country, has strong lines of communication with police and minority group members. The Center is prepared to utilize its own regional field staff in the performance of the study, in collaboration with social scientists, criminologists, and writer-researchers. This will provide us with a mature, skilled group of interviewers and community analysts who will speed the process of locating and hiring staff. Members of CUP's present staff can be temporarily disengaged from their duties and assigned to this study.

Between four and five months after the approval of this project, it is hoped that a preliminary report can be issued which will be duplicated and distributed to police officials, other agencies, and interested groups.

The findings will be made public, and maximum utilization of media and communication will be brought to bear on the problem. The preliminary report will be discussed at national or regional conferences convened by CUP (if appropriate) in collaboration with other groups. On the local level, where police-community relations with minority groups are an important issue, a report will be made available to police officials, as well as local groups. A discussion of the report between police officials and community groups will be encouraged. The academic community will be notified of the findings and additional research will be encouraged. In addition, the report will most likely contain additional research needs. There will be a final report which would be printed and might be used as a manual by police agencies.

Summary of CUP's Experience in Police Training

1. Lloyd Solomon, national program director of the Center on Urban Problems, has been involved in intense study of police-community relations. Several times each year Mr. Solomon lectures to classes of policemen at Walker College in New York City. He is the author of "Study of a Policeman," which has been widely utilized by police de-

partments across the nation. Mr. Walker Oliver, retired police superintendent of the St. Louis Police Department, wrote a foreword to the pamphlet and ordered it mandatory reading for each police officer serving in St. Louis. The Connecticut State Police have included copies of the pamphlet in their daily orders. Mr. Solomon has lectured before the International Association of Police Professors, and has participated in a variety of training seminars.

2. CUP staff assisted the Police Department of New Orleans in the development of an extensive training program involving patrolmen and the communities they serve. CUP staff members helped to devise the program, assisted in writing the grant request which was submitted to the Law Enforcement Administration, and served as consultants to the ongoing program.

3. CUP has published and reprinted a variety of materials suitable for police training purposes. These include pamphlets, books, and films on prejudice and discrimination, civil rights and civil liberties, descriptions of social and cultural life of ethnic minority groups, and analyses of tension situations. Included in CUP's publication list are "A Policeman: A Self Portrait," "Civil Rights and Policemen," and "Policemen's Justice." The last of these was published in cooperation with the Peterson Institute, the International Association of Chiefs of Police, and the Western Center for Human Relations Studies at Omaha University. "A Policeman: A Self Portrait" has sold nearly 100,000 copies. Promotion examinations in the New York City police force have included questions based on this publication.

4. CUP staff has participated in police training and inservice and rookie training programs, and has provided consultation services to such cities as Houston, Tex.; Omaha, Neb.; Los Angeles and San Francisco, Calif.; Atlanta, Ga.; Detroit, Grand Rapids, and Battle Creek, Mich.;

Chicago, Rockford, and Waukegan, Ill.; Indianapolis, Gary, Fort Wayne, and Bloomington, Ind.; Washington, D.C.; Richmond, Va.; and Denver, Colo.

5. CUP staff members have participated in many police conferences. We have been involved as either co-sponsors of or participants in the following:

a. Ohio Conference on "Racial Tension and Law Enforcement"
b. Indiana Conference on Police-Community Relations
c. Annual Police Institute, Buffalo, N.Y.
d. New England Association of Chiefs of Police Training Institutes
e. Police Training Film Conference, New York Police Department
f. Police Executive Conference on Civil Rights, Omaha University
g. Police-Community Relations Workshop, Tower University, Atlanta, Ga.
h. Police Training Institute, Frankfort, Ky.

BUDGET

Project director—six months	$11,000
Travel, per diem, incidentals	3,800
Social scientists' team— five months (part-time)	10,000
Consultant fees and travel for law enforcement reports	15,000
Travel for social scientists	4,000
Three writer-researchers— five months (full- or part-time)	15,000
Travel, etc.	6,000

Temporary replacements for regional
and national CUP staff while they
are allocated to study   12,000

Preparation (editing, duplicating, and
distribution) of preliminary report   4,000

National or regional conferences to
"launch" report   5,000

Preparation and publication
of final report   5,000

                              TOTAL $90,800

RESUMÉS

SELLING YOURSELF IN PRINT

You are a special person. No one else is just like you. Out there somewhere is just the right job for you, and that job is unique in itself. Getting that job is a matter of successfully matching you—one person—to that job—one job. It's like one on one in basketball. And it is not in any way like selling millions of cars or shoes or stereos to millions of people.

What I'm getting at is quite simply this: *Don't use mass-produced resumés!* If you do, you may get 4 interviews (not job offers) per 100 resumés mailed, when you have the potential to get many more. And if your mass-produced resumé is competing in a tough job market, you may get no interviews per 500, 800, or more mailings. I didn't make up these numbers. They come from studies summarized by Richard Nelson Bolles in his popular *What Color is Your Parachute?*[9]

So, how do you sell yourself in print?

The achievement list. As a first step, write down an achievement list. The key word is *achievement.* Not only write down things like job titles or where you went to school, also write down *how well* you performed. And be specific. Use numbers, percentages, dollars. Were you third in your class? In the top two percent? What was your grade point average? How many dollars did you make (or save) for other employers? How efficient were you in terms of time—hours or months—saved on a particular project? How many people did you supervise? What has your promotion record been? Don't write "outstanding." Instead, write (if it's accurate) "level A to level B in so many months, which is X months faster than my contemporaries." You should also make note of awards, scholarships, honors, class offices held, and volunteer work done.

The purpose of the achievement list is to give you a catalog of facts, facts, facts that will answer the employer's question: "How well have you performed in other jobs?" And it's best to try whenever possible to think of your achievements in terms of money, especially profits. The reason for this is obvious: Business exists for only one purpose—to make money.

And keep this list up to date. As you add achievements in your life, add them to the list.

The criteria and goals list.   Your criteria and goals list is next. In it, you answer questions like these: Where do I want to live? Where do I want to work? What do I want to do? What have I liked about past jobs? Disliked about them? What do I want to be doing when I'm 30, 40, 50? Do I want to switch careers? Can I do so without a lot of training? Will I have to go back to school? Do I like working alone? With people? Solving problems? Doing detailed analytical work?

This is a personal list. Only you can answer all of the questions that are on it. But write the answers down. Just having a written plan makes any task easier. Besides, having your criteria and goals in writing where you can refer to them from time to time may keep you from plunging into a job that you really don't want.

Letters and resumés.   Your next step is to work on the writing necessary for a three-phase program:

• Your letter of application. The purpose of this letter is to "tease" the company into inviting you in for an interview so that more can be learned about you.

• Your resumé. You may be asked to bring a resumé to the interview or send one in after.
  Note: Some advisers recommend sending a resumé attached to a cover letter that says something like "please see my resumé attached." If you do, you have now given your reader two pieces of paper to handle instead of one. This reader happens to be the person you're trying to convince to become your next boss. I strongly recommend you make the boss' job as easy as possible. Put your appropriate qualifications into a one-page letter, and make that letter far more interesting and eye-catching than the bunches of two- and three-page packages that your next boss will have to wade through.

• Your follow-up letter. The follow-up letter is perhaps the most neglected of job-search aids.

Whenever you write, try to follow the pointers given here.

1. Lead off with the important item. What's important? The stuff your potential boss wants to hear, and that may not be the same as what you think you ought to write. Remember, the boss wants to hear how you're going to help the company, not "I want this job because it will provide me with a challenge and help me grow." Don't tell the company what it's supposed to do for you. Tell what you can and will do for the company.

2. Slant your language. Aim your words at a particular job. Describe concrete achievements; take them right off your achievement list. Use "power" verbs—*directed, administered, developed, planned, evaluated, originated,* and so on. Avoid shoptalk, and use simple words that read easily. Write in short sentences. It will mean rewriting and rewriting, but short, brisk sentences pull the reader along. When using numbers, write numerals, do not spell out; numerals are eye-catching. Keep paragraph length down, and hold the resumé or letter to one page or two at the most. Don't load the page down with masses of gray; give the reader some attractive white space.

3. Omit vital statistics. Your age, weight, height, and financial and marital status will not get you a job (unless you are applying for something like sheriff or police officer). Furthermore, some questions relating to these may be illegal.

4. Make yourself available. Be certain that whatever you write contains your phone number and address. Tell when you'll be at your home phone or at your office phone.

5. Don't be modest. Telling about your achievements is not boasting or bragging. Besides, if you don't tell about them, who will?

Let's apply these ideas in a response to this ad.

Communications director, national professional association. Responsible for developing, implementing internal/ external PR programs, with help of part-time assistant. Communications degree, three or more years' similar PR experience required. Texas location $16K-$18K annually.[10]

THE LETTER OF APPLICATION

The letter of application does not tell all. Its purpose is to show selection personnel that you are qualified and should be invited in for an interview. Besides, if you tell all in your letter, then what will you have left for an interview or a resumé?

A letter written in answer to this ad is shown next. Before reading the letter, reread the ad and note that the company wants a communicator who can direct and develop programs also. Now note the organizational pattern of the letter. It begins with an attention-getting statement, refers to the ad, describes awards won for writing skills, summarizes experience, mentions education, and ends with a request for an interview.

In my present position, I reduced production costs of our internal newsletter by 17%. I did this while adding features and developing increased reader interest. I mention this as part of my response to your ad in the January 1979 *IABC News*.

Some of my other qualifications are:
- Winner of Ed Press award for writing and editing excellence
- Manage internal/external PR program using print, voice, and visual media (5 years experience to present date)
- Developed external bulletin, circulation of 5,000
- Acted in lead and supervisory role with graphic artists, printers, and writers
- Bachelor's degree in journalism

As my experience indicates, I combine cost consciousness with proven communicative and administrative skills.

I look forward to talking more with you about the position. I can be reached at (000) 000-0000.

THE RESUMÉ

Now comes the resumé. You have been asked to come in for an interview and to bring a resumé. What are you going to put in the resumé?

- Your name, address, and phone number. These must be placed in a prominent place where they can be found without searching.
- A statement of your immediate job objective and your *general* qualifications for this job.
- *Specific achievements* that qualify you to hold this job. Here you can expand on the points made in your letter and add additional points.

- More details on your education.
- Any other achievements that will boost your chances of getting the job.

A sample resumé is shown here.

RESUMÉ

NAME IN CAPITAL LETTERS

Address   Telephone number

objective   Communications management, in an organization looking for increasing internal and external PR activities—especially where broad writing skills and an ability to get things done on time and within the budget are needed.

management   Now manage internal/external PR pro-
experience   gram in nationally known organization. Coordinate on-time production of in-house monthly newsletter (circulation 1,500) and externally distributed monthly bulletin (circulation 5,000). Cut costs 17% on in-house newsletter by encouraging employees to act as unpaid reporters, by using a student intern to design artwork and do paste-up, and by revising typesetting techniques. Title—Director, Office of Information. Length of time—5 years.

writing and   Winner of Ed Press awards (1977, 1978)
editing   for newsletter excellence. Certified as
experience   an Accredited Business Communicator by the International Association of

Business Communicators. Articles published in nationally circulated magazines. Experience as general assignment reporter for leading metropolitan daily paper with circulation of 125,000 —2 years; television news writer for #1 station in 5-channel viewing area—1 year; writer-editor with current company—3 years.

education
Bachelor's degree in journalism. Edited college paper.

other facts
Honored by JayCees for leading 1978 Community Fund drive.

THE FOLLOW-UP LETTER

Regardless of how you feel about the interview and the job, send a follow-up letter. If you want the job, the follow-up puts your name and your abilities in front of the interviewer one more time. And if you don't want the job, well, who knows, you may have second thoughts at a later date.

What goes in a follow-up letter?

- A statement of "thanks for the interview."

- A brief statement that again matches your abilities to the needs of the organization.

- A statement that you will contact the interviewer again in a few days.

A sample follow-up letter is shown here.

Thanks for your time yesterday afternoon. I enjoyed talking with you and meeting other members of your staff.

I'm glad you mentioned budget constraints and limitations on the position. I have proven that I am productive in a no-frills operation, and I believe this type of talent would be an asset to your organization.

I'll get in touch with you again in a few days to discuss the future.

Where do you go from here? To the bibliography of this book. There you will find the books that I have found most helpful in searching for a job. After that, to your local library and a check of the card file for books on resumés, interview taking, vocational guidance, and finding and landing the right job.

II-F.

NEWS RELEASES

A news release is an announcement written to tell the public about an activity of an organization or person. A news release goes from an individual, or public or private agency, to editors in newspapers and radio and television stations. Typical news releases announce: a company's quarterly or year-end financial status, a charity's fund-raising ball, a politician's position on an issue, a government agency's new program, or any of an unlimited number of other events or items.

Your news story is competing for space, and your competitors are reporters, wire services (such as Associated Press, United Press International), and networks (like ABC, CBS, NBC). You have your best chance for success by incorporating into your news release the features described here.

Timeliness.   A news editor might see or hear over a hundred stories a day. All of them—yours included—have some potential news value. But the story that arrives late is just not news.

So, know the deadline. How do you find out? Call the editor and ask. Which editor? Small papers and company newsletters are usually one-editor operations, but large papers may have a string of editors listed in the phone book. In that case, the editor you want has a title like ''City Editor'' or ''Metropolitan Editor.'' With television and radio stations, all that is often listed in the phone book is one number, no string of editors. In that case, ask for the ''News Director,'' ''Public Affairs Director,'' or ''Community Affairs Director.'' And when all else fails, just tell the person answering the phone that you have a news story and you want to know who to tell it to or who to mail it to.

Also, for maximum coverage, choose a release day early in the week. Friday and weekends are slow news days unless your story carries an unusual impact. Then, too, try to get the release out in the morning, before 11 a.m. if possible. That time will give you your best shot at evening TV and the next morning's papers—the biggest news markets.

Substance.   Defining what constitutes news is next to impossible. Textbooks, editors, and reporters never see eye to eye on the subject. Still, you can automatically rule out gossip and stories about corporate crime or bureaucratic boondoggling. If there's any dirty laundry to be hung out, someone else will do it. That leaves good news:

- Accomplishments or activities of the organization, its units, or its programs
- Achievements of employees
- Future events involving the organization
- Important happenings at past events
- Weddings and births involving organization personnel

An exception to the above list is the death of a prominent organization staffer. Even though an item like this is certainly not good news, it usually is reported.

Also, news and publicity are not necessarily the same. If you have loaded your news release with the company name throughout or tried to sneak the company name into seemingly inconspicuous places, you are not writing news; you are advertising. Your "news" release has little chance for success, but you might get a call from the advertising department.

Format.   A news release, such as shown in Figure II-F1, has on it:

- Identification: Organization name and address; contact person and phone number.
- Release time and date: Either "Immediate" or a date is specified.
- Short title: To write a title for your release, take the topic of the story and summarize it in the briefest statement possible.

◢◣ NEWS

from MILES LABORATORIES, INC., Elkhart, Indiana 46514

CONTACT: **Merlin D. Knispel**
(219) 264-8258

FOR RELEASE: **Immediately**

MILES LABORATORIES ANNOUNCES YEAR-END RESULTS

ELKHART, Ind. – February 14, 1978 – Miles Laboratories, Inc., today announced preliminary results for 1977. Net sales reached a new record of $479 million, an increase of 6.5% over 1976. Net earnings, aided by a strong fourth quarter, reached $16.4 million, or $3.03 per share compared to $3.02 per share in 1976.

In announcing these results, Walter Ames Compton, M.D., Chairman and Chief Executive Officer, stated, "Earnings from consolidated operations before income tax actually were up nearly 27% over last year but the reduction of net earnings to near the 1976 level derived principally from higher taxes resulting from revised regulations for handling foreign tax credits. These unused foreign tax credits are available for use during the next five years. The fourth quarter was especially strong with net earnings after taxes up over 23%, or 83¢ per share versus 69¢ last year. These results reflect continuing efforts within the Corporation to improve the margins on our product lines and improve the return on capital employed by the Company.

(more)

Miles Laboratories Announces Year-End Results   Page 2

"Strong gains were reflected in the sales and earnings of our Industrial Products Group as the new citric acid production facility in Dayton, Ohio, reached design capacity in the latter part of the year. The Consumer Products

Group also improved margins in 1977 on a small sales gain.

"As previously announced, the tender offer by Bayer AG for all of the

shares of the Company was successfully concluded in January, 1978, with over

97% of the shares acquired."

II-F1

For instance, the release in Figure II-F1 consists of several paragraphs about year-end financial results, and that's all the title says, ''Miles Laboratories Announces Year-end Results''—five words.

- Dateline: The dateline tells when the event is happening; the editor will more than likely put it somewhere else than the top line of the story.

- Neatly typed, double-spaced or triple-spaced, with wide margins for editor's comments.

- The word *more* typed at the bottom of each page except the last. *More* tells the editor that the story isn't over.

- An ending signature. This is traditional, and the two common ending signatures are:

# # #

or

30

What the release is about. In preparing a news release you should answer as many as possible, if not all, of the six questions of news writing:

- Who?
- Where?
- What?
- Why?
- When?
- How?

The release should answer these questions clearly and quickly. It is not necessary, however, to answer them all in the first paragraph and certainly not in one fact-saturated first sentence.

Lead. The lead (first sentence or paragraph) is perhaps the hardest part of the release to write. The lead must grab the editor's interest. It must have news value. But you shouldn't make the mistake of cramming the *who, when, what, where, why,* and *how* all into one sentence; it's too much for readers to handle. Instead, search for one or two of those ingredients that will appeal to people.

What appeals to people? Well, there's an old axiom that people like stories about other people, conflict, and sex. In business and government journalism, conflict and sex as topics are pretty much out. That leaves us with people as a possible subject for a lead. Another option is to begin with a lead about money, for business profits and government spending (or saving) are always eye-catching news items.

Incidentally, the *when* angle is important, but dates are dull. (Did you like studying history?) In other words, even if a meeting date is important, don't make it the first thing the reader sees. Instead cater to the reader's curiosity by writing about what's going to happen at the meeting. Then give the date.

The lead of the Miles Laboratories' release works well because in one short paragraph it tells a story: Sales and earnings are up. These facts are not loaded into one long sentence. Instead, the writer has given the reader a chance to absorb important information.

This lead also identifies *who* (Miles Laboratories) did *what* (financial results) and *when* (1977). The *how, why,* and *where* are worked into other parts of the release.

Here are two more successful leads:

Ronald E. Waller [who], field services engineer [more on who], recently [when] lost 41 pounds [what] in 17 weeks [more on when] during a successful weight reduction program that involved exercising and proper nutrition [how].

and

Employees [who] in the Wire and Spool Corporation [where] cope with the high price of coffee [what] these days [when] by collecting aluminum cans, selling them to a local aluminum recycler, and using the proceeds to buy coffee for the company's cafeteria [how].

Neither lead answers all of the *who, what, when, where, how,* and *why.* The facts that are needed to answer those questions can be provided in following paragraphs.

After the lead.   After the lead, write up the other aspects of your story. Set up a sequence based on importance. That is, put the most important items near the top of the story and save less significant facts for last. Condense facts into short sentences and paragraphs. Following these instructions will make it easier for an editor to trim your story to fit.

Also, keep the release short. There is rarely any reason for a news release to be longer than two double-spaced pages.

Clear and simple language.   Write the release in clear and simple language. Aim for the general public, not another scientist, doctor, or computer programmer. Avoid acronyms and abbreviations. If you must use them, spell out what they mean the first time you mention them in the text. Keep sentences short, of an average length of around 20 words or less, and avoid complicated sentence structures. Also, translate technical terms into lay language.

When writing the release, use active voice. Say, "the board of directors decided . . ." rather than "it was decided by the board of directors." Active voice puts people up front in the sentence. Active voice shows people doing things, people in charge of issues, and not issues being done by people.

Dialogue.   Someone should appear in your release, be named, and talk. Quotes make a story sound human, and quotation marks catch the reader's eye. Lead off with a quote, if you wish, or sprinkle them throughout the story, but make sure that the reader knows who is talking.

Try to get a quote or quotes from someone important—chief executive officer, chairman of the board, agency director. The more important the person, the more impact the quote and the release will have on the reader.

Problems?   If you have problems getting your news stories run, talk to the editor. A librarian I know took her releases to the editor of a paper in which she wanted publicity. He showed her what he looked for and gave her a short, half-morning course in news release writing. Editors are busy, but they aren't impossible to deal with. And they are on the lookout for news, news from all sources.

II-G.

TECHNICAL WRITING

When you read the owner's manual that comes with a new car, you are reading the work of a technical writer. When you follow the instructions for putting together a tricycle, you are reading the work of a technical writer. When you read an article in a medical journal or a report by one of your organization's engineers, you are reading the work of a technical writer. Technical writing is, indeed, all around us, for we could even say that the authors of science fiction and futuristic novels incorporate technical writing into their works.

Any field this broad is difficult to define in a reasonable number of words. Nevertheless, it is possible to state that technical writing possesses certain identifiable characteristics. Chief among these are the requirements that facts be presented accurately and impartially and with no attempt to arouse emotion. In addition, technical writing relies in large part on a scientific and technical vocabulary and uses frequent visual aids to help clarify difficult concepts. Also, the prose style of most technical writing is more formal than many other styles. As an example, contractions are rarely used in the style that is characteristic of technical writing.

POINT OF VIEW

Technical writing should reflect the objectivity of the scientific approach. Thus, the writing itself should be objective. To some writers, editors, and managers, an objective point of view in writing means a complete absence of personal pronouns such as *I*, *we*, and *our*.

This particular brand of objectivity often results in unhealthy doses of passive voice. Instead of reading about "scientists performing experiments," we read that "experiments were performed." Instead of reading about "people doing research," we are informed that "research was accomplished." Page after page of that kind of writing is a certain cure for insomnia.

Worse, this so-called objectivity in no way guarantees that the report is truly objective. Any reasonably clever writer can slant information any way possible and never once appear in print as *I* or *we*.

Therefore, to help establish a realistic and readable point of view—

- Write in the first person. Use *I* or *we* when appropriate. *I* is appropriate when the point of view is limited to one person: the writer. *We* is appropriate for a group of people: the staff, the company, General Motors. Do not use the editorial *we*, the old-fashioned way of disguising that it is really *I* doing the talking.

- Be modest. Don't shower the page with *I*'s and *we*'s. Once you have established the point of view, it is not necessary to keep reminding the reader.

- Use active voice. Write "I examined the specimens," not "the specimens were examined." Write "General Motors cars do X," not "X is done by General Motors cars."

METHODS OF ANALYSIS

Basic methods of analysis are *classification-partition* and *comparison-contrast*. The techniques are not complex. They require only a brief explanation.

Classification-partition. Begin by identifying a group, say, houses. Next, narrow the group to a subgroup, the units of which all have something in common. You will then have established a classification. For purposes of illustration, you might narrow the group of houses to the subgroup (classification) of Victorians. Next, take a typical Victorian house and describe the components of it. These components need have nothing in common. This is partitioning, and you could literally partition a Victorian house by writing about each of its rooms.

Comparison-contrast. You can compare an item with similar items or contrast it with dissimilar items. The trap to be avoided is the tennis-ball effect in which the reader is bounced back and forth between subjects:

> Fixed-site laboratory equipment is usually large while at the same time relatively fragile as compared to mobile equipment which must be compact and sturdy. Fixed-site equipment generally costs less than comparable mobile lab equipment. Fixed-site equipment offers fewer functions per unit whereas mobile equipment frequently combines multiple functions within a single unit. Fixed-site equipment seems to have a long service life when measured against the relatively short service life of mobile equipment. The power requirements for fixed-site equipment are usually easy to supply, but the power needed to operate mobile lab equipment is not always available.

As a short summary, that wouldn't be too bad. But an entire report, memo, or letter written that way would be deadly. Worse, the tennis-ball effect is often an indication that the writer is not developing individual points.

The failure to develop individual points can be avoided by challenging each statement as you write it down. Ask yourself: "What does my reader need to know here?" "Where does this thought lead to?" Take this sentence:

> The power requirements for fixed-site equipment are usually easy to supply, but the power needed to operate mobile lab equipment is not always available.

That sentence raises these questions: Why is power easy to find for fixed-site equipment? Are electrical outlets always available? Usually available? Is it 110 volt power, 220, or both? Are both needed? Always? Usually? What amperage service is needed? Why is power hard to find for mobile equipment? Is the equipment too far from power lines? Always? Usually? Can portable generators be towed to the site? Are portable generators available? Are they too expensive?

Answer those questions, and you will have developed that one sentence into at least a single, solidly-packed paragraph.

STYLISTIC FAULTS

The stylistic faults described here are *al* and *ly* forms, *exaggeration, absolute generalization,* and *surface reasoning.*

al and ly forms.   What is "an *exceptional* reliability record"? The way that sentence is worded, the reliability record can be exceptionally good or exceptionally bad. Here clarity demands facts, numbers, percents.

How about this one: "This system is more *efficiently* designed than its predecessors." Again, what does *efficiently* mean in terms of cold, hard facts?

Exaggeration.   When we talk, we say things like "thousands of people attended the noon rally in the park [a few hundred were there for the rally; the rest were passing by or just eating lunch in the park]; "the governor made a moving and emotional speech" [only to those who were moved by it]; "and everyone came away impressed" [Everyone? How can we tell?].

Exaggeration in conversation is accepted and understood, but exaggeration in writing may be taken literally with the result that the reader becomes misinformed. The way to avoid exaggeration is to use facts, numbers, and details. And if they aren't available, we should admit that there are limits to what we know about the subject.

Absolute generalization.   Absolute generalization refers to the use of the words *all, right, wrong, true, false, never, always.* These words, if used, must be used with extreme caution. Is it possible to write that "X is always true"? What is probably more correct is that "Evidence gathered up to this time by Y number of people points to X being true under such-and-such conditions."

Surface reasoning.   Here's an example of surface reasoning: "Because the district's personnel change every year or two, no routine inspection program has been established." That's not the whole story, for it might be quite possible to start an inspection program regardless of how often people come and go. The real reasons for the lack of an inspection program could have been one or a combination of these: New employees may not have seen a need for an inspection program; everyone could have been too busy on other projects; no one was interested in an inspection program; or management did not want one. The circumstance of personnel turnover is a surface reason. Write about the real problem.

DEFINING

You have to define words or terms that you believe will be strange to your reader. The standard advice for writing these definitions begins like this:

- Make every effort to state the definition in words that are not part of the term being defined.
- Phrase the definition in predominantly positive terms. You don't get anywhere by telling only what something is not. You must say what it *is*.

After that, whatever works, works. You may relate a thing to others in the same class, discuss its parts, describe what it looks like and how it is used, explain word derivation, or compare it with similar items or contrast it with dissimilar items. You may use a figure, illustration, or photograph; cite an authority (Professor so-and-so says, ". . . ."); or take from a dictionary (According to *Webster's*, ". . . ."). If you do use a dictionary, you owe it to your reader to say which dictionary, for not all dictionaries give identical definitions.

With that advice in mind, what happens if it becomes necessary to write a definition of the term *Christmas tree* as it occurs in Air Force shoptalk?

Well, a dictionary is usually a good starting point, for there is always a chance that the definition is already written down. If your dictionary is anything like the ones convenient to me, however, it's no help here. What I find when I look in three different *Webster's* is that a Christmas tree has something to do with Christmas, forests, oil wells, drag racing, and submarine control panels—but nothing to do with military aviation.

The next steps then would be to look at the Christmas tree in question and to interview flight and ground crews to find out how it is used. When that is done, enough knowledge can be gained to write a basic definition in sentence form:

A Christmas tree is a special parking area set aside for aircraft in a combat-ready configuration. The airplanes are positioned on parking slabs that are joined to each side of a central taxiway and that point to the taxiway at a 30-degree angle. From the air, the slabs resemble branches attached to a trunk (the central taxiway).

That basic definition can now be placed in the report's glossary, used as a footnote, or worked into the text.

A glossary is a wise choice when you have to define a number of terms that will be used throughout the text. Traditionally, the spot for the glossary has been after the text. There is much to be said, though, for placing the glossary in front of the introduction. In that position, the glossary will stand a better chance of being noticed and used by the reader.

In a glossary, terms are arranged alphabetically and are not introduced by a letter or a number. No ending punctuation is needed unless a complete sentence ends the definition. Hanging indentation can be used to make terms stand out:

Christmas tree: a special parking area set aside for aircraft
in a combat-ready configuration. . . .
From the air, the slabs resemble branches attached to
a trunk (the central taxiway).

Terms that are used infrequently or that appear a long distance from the glossary should be defined where they appear. These "spot" definitions can be written as footnotes or worked into the text in a variety of ways:

Combat-ready aircraft are parked in a special area (called a
"Christmas tree") that is made up. . . .

or

Aircraft in a combat-ready configuration are parked on a
Christmas tree—a special area that. . . .

or

Crews call this special parking area a "Christmas tree."
There the airplanes are positioned. . . .

DESCRIBING

For the technical writer, description performs three valuable functions:

- First and most important, description adds proof to scientific writing. It does this by showing that the writer is reporting from firsthand knowledge, that the writer was there. Description makes writing ring true.

- Next, description illustrates. It helps teach the reader by showing how things work and look.
- Also, description adds a touch of literariness to writing. It does this by appealing to the readers' senses and imaginations as well as to their intellects.

Writing good description is much like any other kind of writing. It must be organized, framed in the right words, and then its depth and length must be controlled.

Organization of description. To organize description, it is best to lead the reader into the subject the way you saw it. Give a glimpse first, often no more than a sentence, and then, as you move closer, tear the subject apart and go into details. In the following passage, note how the catalytic converter is first compared to a muffler, a device many people are familiar with, and then described in more depth. An illustration like figure II-G1 can be used to supplement the description.

UNDERFLOOR CATALYTIC CONVERTER

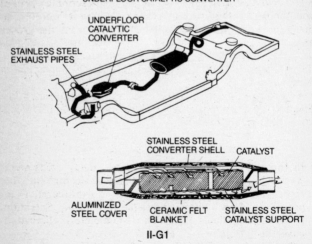

II-G1

The catalytic converter is a small metal cannister that cleans up emissions from automobile exhausts. The converter looks like a muffler and is installed in the car's exhaust system between the engine and the muffler. Converter sizes vary, depending on the size of the engine: the bigger the engine, the bigger the converter.

The converter is filled with either pellets or a honeycomb coated with platinum or palladium. These metals are the catalysts, substances that bring about or hasten chemical changes without changing their own forms.

Hot exhaust gases enter the catalytic converter through an inlet cone and pass over the catalyst. The catalyst then changes carbon monoxide and hydrocarbons into nonpolluting carbon dioxide and water vapor which leave through the outlet cone. In some newer cars, a three-way catalyst is used that also converts oxides of nitrogen into the harmless gases nitrogen and oxygen.

A typical catalytic converter consists of an aluminized steel outer shell, a stainless steel inner shell, a ceramic-felt insulation blanket inside the shell, and interior brackets that support the catalyst. The converter is attached with commonly found fittings, bolts, and nuts; no special tools are needed to remove and replace one.

Describing a process. When you are describing a *process,* you should introduce it by naming it, stating its purpose, and mentioning the chief steps. If a person performs the process, give that person a title: solderer, farmer, gas station attendant, or whatever applies. Next, describe the process from start to finish. As the process is explained, work in the equipment and materials used.

Two sample descriptions of processes are presented here. The first is written for the general reader, the second is intended for a more scientific audience.

BRINGING OIL TO THE SURFACE

In the early days of the oil industry, many wells were wasteful *gushers* that shot oil and natural gas high into the air, sometimes for days. Today, oilmen work carefully to prevent gushers and to control the flow of oil. Scientific production methods have almost completely eliminated gushers.

A driller knows when the bit strikes oil. He examines the drilling mud for traces of it. He also studies the drill cuttings and makes special tests. The drilling crew becomes tense the moment that the bit hits oil. One mistake in bringing in the well may spoil the work of many weeks, and turn a producing well into a dry hole.

After determining that the bit has reached an oil-producing zone, the driller pulls the drill pipe from the hole. Only the casing remains. Usually drillers install an additional casing, called an *oil string* or *production string*, to protect the oil-producing zone from sand and other geological formations exposed during drilling. If the oil string ends above the production zone, drillers sometimes install a long piece of pipe called a *liner* that runs from the bottom of the casing to the production zone. The liner has many holes in it. Finally, a smaller pipe called the *tubing* is lowered into the well. The tubing extends from the liner to the surface of the ground. Oil goes through the holes in the liner and up the tubing to the surface.[11]

BENTHIC STUDY

The bottom half of 9-cm plastic petri dishes were perforated using a 1.6-mm drill. The dishes were filled to within 2 mm of the top with basin soil or clean sand as the substrate for the benthic organisms. For the basin soil substrate, the soil was taken from the depression made in the soil when placing the dishes in position in the study grid. The sand substrate was a mixture of 38 percent 1,000 to 500 μm sand, 47 percent 500 to 250 μm sand, and 15 percent 250 to 125 μm sand. This sand mixture approximated the hydraulic properties of the sandy soil at the study sites. One study site was in the center of the south half of 3A basin, called the central grid, where 20 soil and 20 sand petri dishes were alternated one meter apart in a nearly square grid pattern. The other study site was along the east shore of the 3A basin using 20 soil and 20 sand petri dishes in a 4- by 10-dish grid pattern with 60 cm between dishes. The petri dishes were set out February 6, 1975, and covered with the petri dish lid and a rock to hold the lid on during filling of basin. Most of the petri dishes at the east side off-shore grid were soon lost to wave action. Thus, only grab samples of bottom soil were collected at the east side grid after May. After the basin was filled with water, the dish tops were removed. The depth of the water over the dishes at the central grid ranged between 30 and 45 cm during recharge. The petri dishes and water samples were collected using a boat.

Two soil and sand substrate petri dishes were randomly collected every fourth week during the 1975 recharge period. At sampling time, a petri dish lid was placed over the bottom half, and a metal plate was shoved under the dish. The plate and dish were carefully lifted out of the water. The water was allowed to seep out the bottom of the perforated dish as the soil sample was transported back to the laboratory. One-third of each sample was passed through stacked 500-μm and 20-μm sieves to sample for macrobenthic organisms. Another third was mixed with filtered basin water and was placed in a glass petri dish. This portion was immediately subsampled for microbenthic organisms. Subsampling consisted of placing a small amount of soil or sand substrate in a beaker, mixing it with basin water, stirring vigorously, and pouring off the water and organisms after the heavy soil particles had settled. This process was repeated several times until no more organisms were collected. The third portion of soil or sand substrate was ovendried (105° C) for carbon and nitrogen analysis. Basin water for the benthic study was sampled every 2 weeks for chemical quality parameters at the grid sites and at the inlet to the 3A basin.[12]

Describing an object.   When you are describing an *object,* begin by naming it and stating its purpose. Then, give the reader a look at the object. This first look is often a simile or an analogy, both of which are discussed later in this section. Next, show the object part by part. Explain such items as each part's size, shape, relationship to other parts, method of attachment, material, finish, and color. Two sample descriptions of objects are presented here.

HAMMERS

Hammers are made in many sizes and shapes to handle the multitude of jobs assigned to them. The basic type, of course, is the claw hammer. The head is metal, the handle wood. But even claw hammers vary in shape, and also in quality. The claw may be sharply curved, in which form its major function is to pull out nails, or nearly straight, a variation which not only pulls nails but also separates boards which have been nailed together. This type can be used to split boards along the grain.

The metal head may be cast iron, which is quick and easy

to make. But since cast iron breaks on impact, the best head is made of drop-forged steel, which is practically indestructible. Straight-grained hickory is best for the handle and will last a lifetime if protected against dry rot with linseed oil and against gouges and saw cuts while on the job.

The handle is inserted in a hole in the head, and one or more wedges are driven down into the grain end of the handle, expanding it tightly into the head so that it can't fly off.[13]

MODEL COTTON BALE PRESS

It was felt that the model bale press at the U. S. Cotton Ginning Research Laboratory, Stoneville, Miss., could be used to develop detailed qualitative information relative to the force required to compress lint cotton, and would require substantially less cotton than a full-size press. The model press box has a cross-sectional area of 144 square inches, as compared to a full-size press box, which ranges from 1,025 to 1,475 square inches, and is 70 inches deep, or approximately the same depth as a full-size press box. Test lots of approximately 15 pounds are required for the model bale press, which means that the model bale press requires only 3 percent as much cotton as in the full-size system. A 55-gallon-per-minute hydraulic pump driven by a 50-horsepower electric motor develops compressive force in the model press system. The hydraulic system develops pressure on an 8⅛-inch-diameter, up-packing ram.[14]

Concluding a description. Sometimes a conclusion is added. The main points that will help the reader in the conclusion are reviews of the object's or process' chief features and good and bad points. If a conclusion for a description of an object is written, it helps to show the reader how the object is used; this is actually a brief description of a process. The earlier description of a hammer ends with a description of the process of using a hammer:

A hammer is designed with a definite "balance." That is, maximum impact is provided if the hammer is held properly—at the curved indentation in the handle near its heavy end—and freely swung instead of jabbed at a nail. Wherever possible, arrange your work to use a hammer in this way and you will be amazed at the ease with which the job gets done.

For tight corners and overhead work, of course, this method isn't always possible. Vary the grip if the position demands it. It is important that the exact center of the hammer face strikes the nail on the head and that the direction of the blow is exactly in line with the direction of the nail.[15]

The language of description. To write description, use concrete words that appeal to the senses. For instance, it is not good description to look at a puddle of highly flammable fluid on a service station ramp and then tell the reader that the puddle was caused by a ''product'' leak when the right word is *gasoline. Product* is a vague word; there are many, many products. But *gasoline* is a concrete word. Gasoline is wet and has odor and taste. Readers can see gasoline, and they can touch it. It leaves a pungent odor in the nostrils and a bitter aftertaste in the mouth.

A solid aid to descriptive language is the use of a *simile* or an *analogy*. A simile says that one thing is like another in one respect and uses words like *as* or *like*. An analogy notes several points of comparison:

Simile: To the casual observer, coke looks like coal.

Analogy: A beginning understanding of electrical current flow can be had by comparing electricity to ordinary household plumbing. In this comparison, a difference in pressure sends water through pipes, while a difference in voltage draws current through wires.

For the skeptical (and engineers and scientists are by training distrustful of similes and analogies), let's make these points. Similes and analogies are not statements of fact, they are not evidence, and they are not proof. Nevertheless, similes and analogies are excellent devices for taking the reader across the gap from known to unknown. The differences, the details, the precision—the whole truth—can be fleshed in once that gap is bridged.

Sometimes, the gap is small, and the writer may wonder to what extent a familiar object or process should be described. Answer: Describe only the differences. As an example, if you have to write a description of a lawn mower, don't waste your time and your reader's time by building the mower from the grass up. Just say how this particular lawn mower is different.

Knowing your audience will help you decide how much detail to put into a description. As an example, it is not necessary to describe a welding torch to an audience of welders. But it is necessary to describe a welding torch in an article or book intended for a general audience of do-it-yourselfers.

Verb tense.   Verb tense in descriptive language sometimes poses problems. For technical writers, these problems can be resolved by keeping in mind that present tense is used for permanent truths. That is, if an object always looks a certain way or if a process always works a certain way, then describe it in present tense. Past or future tenses are used to describe differences from permanent truths.

Depth (length) of description.   Deciding when to stop describing is difficult, often especially so for scientists and engineers. The rest of us look at a painting and see frame and subject. The scientific mind sees more: canvas, brushes, numbers, angles, and costs. So the question is, Should you give your reader only a quick look at what you are describing, or should you delve into the numbers and relationships of such things as measurements, angles, temperatures, weights, and velocities? A way out of this predicament is to establish two levels of description, the *pictorial* and the *numerical*. With these terms in mind:

• Always paint a picture, well written, in plain English, so that a reader can see what the subject is.

• Include only those numerical details that are essential to the reader's understanding of the points you wish to make.

INSTRUCTING

When writing instructions, give step-by-step, omission-free directions in the right order. Make that a rule to follow and to carry over from chapter to section to paragraph to sentence. Nothing is worse than instructions given out of sequence. Suppose a writer told how to change oil in this manner: "Drain the oil from the engine after placing a pan under the crankcase." The sequence is wrong. Somewhere out there is an impatient reader who (1) will read no more than the first half of that sentence and (2) will drain oil onto the driveway.

Language for giving directions. When giving directions, use words that tell the reader to perform necessary steps or words that suggest optional ones:

TELL	SUGGEST
Place the pan under the crankcase before draining the oil. Once the pan is in place, remove the drain plug.	After the crankcase is filled, the old oil should be recycled. This can be done by taking the oil to a collection center.

Do not fall back on the language of suggestion because of the theory that it is the polite way to get people to do things. Granted, not all directions can be given in the military manner: "Do this." "Do that." Still, the language of suggestion leaves the reader wondering: "Must I do this?" "Can I get out of that?" It is a point worth stressing: The unnecessary use of words like *should, may be,* and *can be* encourages steps, often critical ones, to be omitted.

And what do you do if policy or equipment design dictates the language of suggestion? In these cases, suggest, but give examples of what can go wrong if your advice is not followed.

Some other pointers are: Instructions are easiest to follow if they are given in short bursts of plain English. In other words, don't load up long sentences with complex ideas and shoptalk. Also, make clear at the start what tools and materials are required. Finally, make certain your reader is informed of any hazards, warnings, or cautions that are associated with the instructions.

III.

A REVIEW OF GRAMMAR AND USAGE

"The question is," said Alice, "whether you *can* make words mean so many different things." "The question is," said Humpty Dumpty, "which is to be master—that's all."

Lewis Carroll (*Through the Looking-Glass*)

God is a verb.

R. Buckminster Fuller
("No More Secondhand God")

III-A.

WORDS

We can inform our readers best if we use words that are familiar, specific, standard, and say what we mean.

Prefer the familiar to the unfamiliar. Familiar words are those the reader has seen time and time again and knows on sight. Familiar words save the reader the trouble of reaching for the dictionary or trying to decode what was in the writer's mind. This short list shows some of the differences.

Unfamiliar	Familiar
conflagration	fire
disincentive	penalty
hegemony	leadership
homologous	alike
metamorphosis	change
pervasively	throughout
ubiquitous	widespread

Prefer the specific to the abstract. Specific words name things individually, one at a time, like *half-ton* truck, *Mount Everest, Convention Center* building, *Black and Decker radial arm* saw. Abstract words name intangible conditions, qualities, or ideas, such as *beauty, culture, efficiency, loyalty, wealth.* Specific words are easy for the reader's mind to work with, for the concepts involved are simple and narrowly defined. Abstract words are hard for the reader's mind to handle, for the things abstract words stand for have no existence outside whatever existence the reader gives them.

Prefer the old standards. This is another way of saying, "Do not use vogue words." Vogue words come and go, and what's in vogue as I write this may not be in vogue when you read it. Here are just a few that are popular today, but tomorrow, who knows? *Breakthrough, comfortable* (It's possible to be comfortable in a chair, but what does it mean to be comfortable in a job? In government?), *conceptual, holistic, interface, meaningful, ongoing, structured* (structured interview, structured feedback), *systems approach* (systems approach to design, to training), *the bottom line, viable.*

Say what is meant. When something was *connected,* was it welded, soldered, spliced, or bolted? When an experiment is *checked,* is it verified, stopped, inspected, marked with a check, or left in the checkroom? Also, don't *transfer* liquids; pour or pump them. Don't *examine* a sample; smell it or dissect it.

Two do's. Do use a scientific word when that's the best word to describe what you mean. There's a lot of advice in this book about short words and familiar words. But you should disregard that advice when a long scientific word is the only word that will work.

For instance, if a writer casually writes about fish, the marine biologist will not know whether the subject is *osteichthyes* (bony fishes) or *chondrichthyes* (fish with cartilage for skeletons). If we write of alcohol, the chemist will wonder if we are talking about *ethyl* alcohol or *methyl* alcohol, the two most popularly known types, or over a dozen others with names like *isopropyl* alcohol, *isobutyl* alcohol, or *ethylene glycol.*

In conversation and in much general writing, the more common term may suffice. But scientific and technical writing demand that the exact word be used.

Also, do develop a questioning attitude. Challenge every word. You'll increase your vocabulary and become more confident in your ability to use words. Keep a thesaurus or synonym finder close by, and use a dictionary frequently. But don't buy a third-rate one. Book titles are not copyrighted, and anyone can put out a *Webster's.* The dictionaries I recommend are listed in the bibliography.

Become sensitive to changes in meaning. Words change meaning. Think of words that have changed meanings recently.

One is *energy,* a "small" word at one time, a personal word having something to do with how you felt. Now, *energy* can refer to the decline of civilization. For the writer, this shift in emphasis points to a need to use words with accurate meanings and in the appropriate contexts—to be ever alert.

Finally, don't be embarrassed by having to "look it up." Professional editors and writers have dictionaries at their elbows and scattered around their offices and homes. The pros know the value of a dictionary. You should too.

Problem words.   The following words are frequently misused. Guidance for proper use accompanies the offenders.

Affect, effect. To solve the problems connected with *affect* and *effect,* rely on this pattern:

BEFORE	DURING	AFTER
Effect (verb)	Affect (verb)	Effect (noun)
to bring about,	to influence	consequence,
to cause to		result
come into being		

But be careful. There are differences between the *affects* (influences) and the *effects* (consequences) of government spending. When in doubt, abandon *affect, effect* and use the right synonym.

Alternate, alternative. Alternate refers to one after the other; *alternative,* to one or the other (or more possibilities).

Among, between. Use *between* when referring to two persons or objects; use *among* when referring to three or more: *"Between* innings the players on the losing team argued *among* themselves."

As, like. Use *as* to join clauses: "This month was warm, *as* should be expected." Use *like* to compare nouns: "June is warm *like* May."

Assure, ensure, insure. Are you unsure about when to use *assure, ensure,* or *insure?* If so, consult either the *Webster's New Collegiate Dictionary* (Springfield, Massachusetts: G. & C. Merriam Company, 1977) or the *Webster's New World Dictionary* (2d college ed. New York: William Collins & World Publishing Company, 1974)—and you will be more unsure. The *New World* gives what I believe are the popularly assumed differences: *Assure* pertains to making a person sure of something; *ensure,* to make certain in general; and *insure,* to money to be paid in case of loss. But the *New Collegiate* does not fully support these differences and in fact can be read as treating the three words as synonyms. Here is one instance where a writer, to be secure, can literally go shopping for definitions.

Because, since. *Since* is often used in a sentence involving a time element: "Since 1933, when prohibition ended. . . ." Also, authors have been using *since* to mean *because* for five centuries. What is needed, then, is a workable practice for separating the two. Such a practice would involve restricting *because* to causal situations, for just the sight of the word plants the notion of cause rather than time in the reader's mind. Justification for such a rule can be found in sentences like this:

> Since your garage worked on my car, I have had to fix the brakes.

What does that sentence mean? I don't know, for two meanings are possible: (1) since the date your garage worked on my car . . . or (2) because your garage worked on my car and botched it up. . . . The use of *since* leaves the reader in doubt.

Cheap, inexpensive. The difference between *cheap* and *inexpensive* demonstrates what is known as the difference between the denotative and connotative value of words. Both *cheap* and *inexpensive* denote something that doesn't cost much. Additionally, *cheap* carries with it the connotation of shabby merchandise. An *inexpensive* test gauge may last a long time. A *cheap* one probably won't.

Comprise. *Comprise* means "to include; to contain." A state can *comprise* counties and irrigation districts, but none of these can *comprise* a state.

Continuous. *Continuous* means "going on without interruption or break." No one monitors any process *continuously.*

Feel. Avoid using *feel* to mean "think" or "believe." If we write, "We *feel* Stage III will accomplish its purpose," we are indicating that we have stopped thinking and are guided by instinct or sense of touch. Our position will sound more positive if we write, "We think," "the staff believes," or "our opinion is."

If, whether. Use *whether* (usually with *or*) when presenting alternatives; use *if* when attaching conditions to a statement.

> Conditions: If the day is nice, we'll have a picnic.
> Alternatives: . . . did not know whether to go or to stay.

Data. The word *data* is often used in speech as a singular noun. Also, common usage often treats *data* as a collective noun like *group* or *orchestra*. Thus many people write of *data* as being singular: the *data* is; the *group* is; the *orchestra* is.

But as long as *datum* (standard datum plane) exists as the true singular, then *data* is the plural form. Thus, there is no getting out of correcting the examples on the left:

WRONG	RIGHT
This is current *data*.	*These are* current *data*.
For *this data* to be useful, *it needs* to be available on a timely basis.	For *these data* to be useful, *they need* to be available on a timely basis.

Incidentally, an easy way to cope with *data* is to mentally substitute the word *numbers* for *data* as you write. The plural sound of *numbers* will help lead you to the correct verb form.

Imply, infer. These two words apply to opposite ends of the same process. *Imply* refers to the sending end, *infer* to the receiving end. When you talk to someone, you may *imply* (hint at) a certain meaning, but that person may *infer* (derive) a different meaning. One device that may help in this instance is to remember that the last letter of *infer* is the same as the first letter of *receive*.

Only. *Only* must be placed next to the term it modifies. Note the shift in meaning in these sentences as *only* is moved.

I calculated *only* the company's balance sheet.
I calculated the *only* company's balance sheet.
I calculated the company's *only* balance sheet.
I calculated the company's balance sheet *only*.

Oversight. When *oversight* first came into the language, it was used to mean "the action of overseeing," that is, supervising, managing, controlling, or inspecting. Later, *oversight* picked up a totally different meaning: "the act of passing over without seeing," that is, omission, failure, or mistake. The best bet here is say exactly what is meant and avoid the confusion that *oversight* presents.

Provided, providing. Careful usage dictates a difference between *provided* and *providing:* "The 95 percent criterion can be met by use of the new system, *provided* (only if) the system is operated by trained personnel"; "In the spring, insulation and up-valley winds increase *providing* (giving) better ventilation."

Second, secondarily. *Second* points to the second item in a series; that item may be just as important as the first. *Secondarily* refers to an item below the first in rank or importance.

That, which. *That* is best used to introduce an essential sentence element (word, phrase, or clause), and *which* is best used to lead into a nonessential element.

Essential: The river that flows into Folsom Lake is low this year. (Try removing *that flows into Folsom Lake*, and the river is no longer identified.)

Nonessential: The American River, which flows into Folsom Lake, is low this year. (*Which flows into Folsom Lake* is not needed to identify the river.)

A reasonable question is, Why use *that* for essential information and *which* for nonessential? One answer can be found in dictionaries. Dictionaries are basically history books that report on centuries of usage. According to dictionary definitions and examples, a *that-which* "code" has existed for a long time. Using the *that-which* code gives us a device in addition to the comma (the weakest of marks) to tell the reader what kind of information is coming. Then, too, *that* sounds harsher than *which*, plays louder on the reader's ear, and sends a stronger signal that important (essential) information is coming.

While. While is primarily thought of as having a meaning or a sense that pertains to time. Thus, "*While* the rest played cards, he studied" tells the reader that two actions took place at the same time. *Although* can be substituted for *while* in that sentence without violating any principles of grammar: "*Although* the rest played cards, he studied." But now the time element is absent, and *although* is not a satisfactory substitute as to meaning.

Then there is this misuse of *while:* "The early morning will be cold, *while* afternoon temperatures will rise to near seasonal norms." Why not *but?*

Abbreviations.   If you have to use an abbreviation, explain it to your reader. The usual method is to write the term out in full and then show the abbreviation in parentheses: "Did you know that there are over a dozen organizations that use the same abbreviation as the American Medical Association (AMA)?" In a short document the parenthetical definition need be given only once, the first time it occurs. In a document of several chapters or several hundred pages, it is wise to redefine abbreviations the first time they occur in each chapter.

The tendency to use abbreviations is strong but should be avoided whenever possible. The reliance on too many abbreviations results in a cluttered look on the pages. In addition, the reader is forced at each abbreviation to slow down and decode the letters.

Three abbreviations that should be especially avoided are *e.g.*, *i.e.*, and *etc*. Many readers and writers confuse the first two. To set the meanings straight here, *e.g.* means "for example," and *i.e.* means "that is." As for *etc.*, it can be done away with by using *such as* or *including:* "Internal combustion engines come in a variety of types, *such as* reciprocating and turbine."

Also, it is not necessary to write *Inc.* after a company's name. Almost all companies are incorporated, and *Inc.* adds nothing worthwhile.

Words and phrases to avoid.   The words and phrases in the left column below have shorter or simpler substitutes that are given in the right column. These are only a few samples, but the principles involved can be applied to other useless words and phrases.

INSTEAD OF	TRY
absolutely essential	essential
activate	begin
actual experience	experience
aggregate	total
analyses were made	analyzed
assist	help
beyond a shadow of a doubt	undoubtedly
communicate	write, tell
demonstrate	show
despite the fact that	although
discontinue	stop
during the time that	while
encounter	meet
endeavor	try
excellent	(a superlative; do not use)
exceptional ability	(define *exceptional* with facts, numbers, statistics)
exhibits a tendency to	tends
facilitate	ease, simplify
few in number	few
field of economics	economics
for the reason that	for
give encouragement to	encourage

he is of the opinion	he thinks
in a number of cases	sometimes
in compliance with your request	as you asked
initial	first
initiate	begin
in the event that	if
in the majority of instances	often
in the nature of	like
in the neighborhood of	about
make representation with	meet with
make an adjustment in	adjust
modification	change
of a confidential nature	confidential
of sufficient materiality	enough
outstanding	(a superlative; do not use)
past history	history
perform an examination	examine
preparatory to	before
present a conclusion	conclude
prior to	before
range all the way from	range from
red in color	red
subsequent to	after
ten miles distant from	ten miles from
terminate	end, stop
the undersigned	I
the writer	I
this office has initiated	we have begun
this point in time	now
three hours of time	three hours
under date of	dated
until such time that	until
utilize	use
we deem it advisable	we suggest
we will endeavor to ascertain	we will try to find out
with regard to	regarding
with this in mind, it is clear that	therefore
years of age	years old
you will find enclosed	here is

Pronoun problems.   Make a pronoun agree with its noun:

DISAGREE	AGREE
Porter Oil (singular) has applied for a permit. *They* (plural) feel a permit should be granted.	*Porter Oil* (singular) has applied for a permit. The *company* (singular) feels a permit should be granted.

Do away with weak pronoun references:

WEAK	STRONG
Prepare a pre-fire plan, train your family in safe home evacuation, and conduct realistic fire drills in the home. *It* could save your lives.	Prepare a pre-fire plan, train your family in safe home evacuation, and conduct realistic fire drills in the home. *These steps* could save your lives.

Word order.   When words are not in the right order, meaning is not clear:

UNCLEAR	BETTER
As we interpret procedure 417, whenever possible, indexing should be based on International Standard Book Numbers. (What part of the sentence does *whenever possible* modify?)	As we interpret procedure 417, indexing should be based on International Standard Book Numbers whenever possible.
The department took an inventory during the week that disclosed a shortage of parts. (Sounds like the week disclosed a shortage of parts.)	During the week, the department took an inventory that disclosed a shortage of parts.

Shoptalk and the plain English style.   You can pick up any number of books or articles that tell you, "Don't write jargon" or "Don't expect your reader to understand shoptalk." That's good advice.

But how—and here's the hard part—are you going to recognize what is shoptalk and what is not? After all, the shoptalk of your profession is your primary language for at least eight hours a day. Your use of shoptalk has probably become deep-seated. Besides, shoptalk does have its good features. A single word in shoptalk will often convey to a colleague what would require a sentence or perhaps pages to convey to a layman. Also, shoptalk is useful when writing in lab or field notebooks or for preparing documents that are intended to go no farther than the files.

Furthermore, shoptalk is English, isn't it? Well, it is and it isn't. A child in elementary school learns that *hydro* means "water" and can be combined with other words to say something about how water is used: hydroelectric power; hydrotherapy. However, a chemist thinks of *hydro* in terms of its being part of the word *hydrogen*. Now suppose the child grows up to be a lawyer and reads a report in which the chemist has used and not defined the word *hydrodesulfurization*. The natural link in the mind of the nonchemist is that sulfur can be removed with water—and that's not what the chemist meant at all.

What each of us needs is a finely tuned filter in the mind that from the start of our careers will sort out the bits and pieces of shoptalk from the mainstream of good standard English.

To construct this filter, you must develop a respect and an ear for the plain English style. The plain English style is a beautiful style. It has been around for centuries and will outlast all the bafflegab, bureaucratese, and gobbledygook we can ever conspire to invent.

You can develop this ear for style by listening to the words you use when you talk and by watching your audience. A suddenly raised eyebrow or tilted head may be a sign that you have turned loose of a word that somebody out there does not understand.

Another step is to make a list of no more than 50 words that are shoptalk in your profession. You don't have to include definitions. All you want is a list of "signal" words that at some later time you may have to define for your readers. Sometimes it's not even necessary to develop the list; you might find it in the glossaries of your textbooks.

Also, read widely, inside and outside your profession. Look closely at how publications like *Time,* the *Reader's Digest,* and the *Wall Street Journal* handle the concepts and terminology of your field. Watch for the way writers define complex terms or present difficult ideas. Note how these professional writers take the shoptalk of your field and convert it to the plain English style.

When you can do that, you will avoid writing passages like:

The influx and distribution of solar energy gives rise to the climates that prevail on Earth. It powers the movement of global air masses, the hydrologic cycle, ocean currents. It provides conditions essential to the life on Earth.[1]

And instead write:

The sun controls our climate, our wind, our rain, our ocean currents. The sun gives us life.

The truth is, it's possible to put anything into plain English, if you work hard enough at it.

III-B.

VERBS

Why one section just on verbs? Because verbs are the action words of the language. Verbs are the *do* words. Verbs put movement and vigor into prose, and the skillful use of verbs can make even the dullest subject readable. Therefore, verbs deserve all the attention we can give them.

ACTIVE VERSUS PASSIVE VOICE

Voice is the term we use to describe a verb form as being either active or passive.

In *active voice*, a force acts upon an object. The force appears first in the sentence:

Active: The woodsman [force] felled the tree [object].

In *passive voice*, an object appears first in the sentence and is then acted upon by a force:

Passive: The tree [object] was felled by the woodsman [force].

Passive voice can also be identified by its reliance on verb forms such as *is, is being, was, were, will be, has been, have been,* and *had been*.

Many writers and teachers say that passive voice is bad, that it adds length to writing, that it confuses the reader—that it is just plain weak prose. Each of these complaints is valid, but before we say why, let's take a look at just what is so good about active voice.

The case for active voice.   As schoolchildren we began our reading lessons with primers in which active voice described the action: "Dick and Jane went to the store," not "The store was where Dick and Jane went." Thus, we took our basic training in reading, and soon writing, in active voice.

Also, our lives are filled with people who *do* things. We see people drive cars, ride bikes, play golf, swim, run, exercise. We read of people who fly space ships, build bridges, and rob banks. People are active, and we think it natural to read a sentence about a woodsman who felled a tree, but it jolts us to read that the tree was felled by a woodsman.

As a result our senses tell us that active voice is right and that passive voice is unnatural. Our senses are right. The active verbs do sound more natural, especially in sentences like this:

Active: We enjoyed the music.
Passive: The music was enjoyed by us.

We are used to the who-does-what sequence. We can follow an account easily if we focus first on the force or persons at work and then on the work they do. In short, active voice is in most cases the way we think. Because of this, and to repeat a point, the passive voice can make it hard for a reader to visualize actions or events.

The case against passive voice.   Here are some complaints against passive voice.

Complaint #1: Passive voice makes for weak prose. That it does, based on the sequence-of-events argument just presented. Then, add to that the dictum that active voice is more vigorous, as can be seen by these comparisons:

Active: Failing health compelled him to leave college.
Passive: The reason he left college was that his health had failed.

Active: Dead leaves covered the ground.
Passive: A great number of dead leaves were lying on the ground.

Complaint #2: Passive voice is confusing. It is sometimes, especially in sentences like the following:

Passive: A survey was made by the department of health of the nursing service at Northern State Hospital.

Who is doing what in the above sentence? In active voice all doubts are removed:

Active: The department of health surveyed the nursing service at Northern State Hospital.

Complaint #3: Passive voice adds length to writing. It does. Look back at the samples. In each case the sentence written in active voice is shorter than the one in passive voice. Brevity is a by-product of writing in active voice.

The case for passive voice.   A controlled use of passive voice can add variety and emphasis to your writing.

For instance, passive voice can be used to move the important element to the front of the sentence. Here the element will receive initial emphasis and catch the reader's eye quicker:

Passive: The President was bitten by a dog.

Passive: Any employee who violates this rule will be discharged.

The passive voice is often used when the originator or the performer of the action is hard to identify or not to be named:

Passive: Some of his brain cells were damaged when he was a child.

Passive: Your driving privilege was suspended under the provisions of the Vehicle Code.

A caution.   The real danger is in the excessive use of passive voice. Passive voice should be the exception in our writing and not the rule, because good writing shows the same vigor that life does. Vigorous prose adds movement to writing and can keep the reader turning pages—and that, after all, is what the writer is supposed to do.

SUBMERGED VERBS

Certain verb forms are submerged; the real action is hidden from the reader. One in that category is the *to be* form. Note the weaknesses that *to be* puts into the samples on the left below. By purging the *to be*s, the sentences become stronger, more direct.

To Be Form	Stronger Form
Discussion centered on a permit updating system *to be* associated with an annual compliance inspection program.	Discussion centered on *associating* a permit update system with an annual compliance inspection program.
The temporary permit is good for up to one year and is *to be* replaced within that period by a long-term permit.	The temporary permit is good for up to one year and *must be* replaced within that period by a long-term permit.

Another form of the submerged verb is the verb that a writer turns into a noun. When that happens, the action disappears from the sentence, and extra words are added. In addition, there is a difference in meaning. The noun form implies an action already completed; the verb form implies an action in progress.

In the samples below, the nouns are italicized and shown in the left column. The column on the right shows the nouns brought to the surface as verbs. Note how each rewritten example on the right is shorter than its original.

Submerged Verbs	Surfaced Verbs
by the *maintenance* of records	by *maintaining* records
difficulties in the *administration* of	difficulties in *administrating*
a *resumption* of operations will	*resuming* operations will
the *elimination* of these expenses shows	*eliminating* these expenses shows
a *reduction* of operating costs can	*reducing* operating costs can

Here's still another weak verb form that can be made stronger:

Weak	Stronger
His testimony *related* to the proposed legislation.	He *testified* about the proposed legislation.

TROUBLESOME AUXILIARIES

The auxiliary verbs to be discussed here are *shall* and *should*, *will* and *would*, *can* and *could*, and *may* and *might*. These verbs are often troublesome because most of us don't write the way we talk. In our speech, which is informal, we tend to be casual with the auxiliaries. Instead of issuing commands by announcing "You shall complete project X," we politely say "You should complete project X." Nevertheless, there is a difference in meaning, and knowing this difference is important for the business writer who must write rules, regulations, and policy directives. Therefore, our best guides are the most formal and the most traditionally correct usages.

Let's begin with the one usage that seems designed for the sole purpose of making English more complicated: When expressing determination use *will* for the first person and *shall* for the second and third persons. Do the reverse when expressing futurity:

FUTURITY	DETERMINATION
I (we) shall	I (we) will
You will	You shall
He (she) (they) will	He (she) (they) shall

After that example, the rest is easy. The rest is especially easy if you take the eight auxiliaries and line them up in the order given in the first sentence of this section. What you will have then is a range of meaning from which you can select the right word to express doubt or choice. *Shall* is the only word at the mandatory end, while at the other end, in the swamp of greatest doubt, is *might*. Such a scale is incorporated into Table III-B1.

Two notes of caution accompany the table.

First, although the tense for each verb is given, it is given only as a guide for matching the auxiliary with other verbs. Otherwise, too much thought about verb tense in these cases can be unnecessary and confusing. For instance, "I *may* (present tense) go to the store tomorrow" and "I *might* (past of *may*) go to the store tomorrow" are both statements made in the present about the future. The difference that counts is not one of tense but one of meaning: *Might* is more conditional than *may*.

Second, the table has been planned to treat only the degrees of doubt or choice that can be read into the auxiliaries. Don't expect it to answer all the questions and solve all the problems the auxiliaries pose.

TABLE III-B1

SOME AUXILIARY VERBS AND THEIR SHADES OF MEANING

THE VERB (AND ITS TENSE)	THE USER (AND THE USE)	AN EXAMPLE (AND ITS TRANSLATION)
Shall (present)	Laws, regulations, contracts, directives (to state what is mandatory)	The employer shall provide proper safety equipment. (Do it!)
Should (past)	Company president to the 1st v.p. (to express an obligation, duty, or what is probable or expected)	We should provide proper safety equipment. (We all know what the law says, but saying and doing are different things.)
	or	
	Company president to the 1st v.p. (to request or suggest in a polite manner; to soften a direct statement)	You should look into providing proper safety equipment. (That's not really a direct order, but if you know what's good for you, you'll do it.)
Will (present)	The 1st v.p. to plant personnel (to express anything from desire, wish, capability, determination, and inevitability to what is mandatory)	Listen up everyone. We will provide proper safety equipment. (Man, that sounded great. But is it actually going to happen?)
Would (past)	The 1st v.p. to the company treasurer	We would provide proper safety equip-

The verb (and its tense)	The user (and the use)	An example (and its translation)
	(to express wish, desire, plan, intention, choice, doubt, or uncertainty; conditions are attached and stated or implied)	ment if funds were available. (Ah, we can always fall back on the old don't-have-the-money excuse.)
Can (present)	The foreman to the director of safety (to express ability)	We can provide proper safety equipment. (There is a place to install it.)
Could (past)	The foreman to the director of safety (to express ability with conditions attached)	We could provide a place for the safety equipment if we redesigned the line. (It's possible, but there is a problem.)
May (present)	Company treasurer to all involved (to give permission)	You may begin installing the safety equipment. (Here's the money. Go to it.)
	or	
	Company treasurer to all involved (to show what is in some degree likely)	You may get your safety equipment when the new budget goes through. (Nothing's definite yet.)
Might (past)	Two line employees, six months later (to show less probability than *may*)	That new safety equipment might be in next week. (Sure. They've been telling us that for months.)

TROUBLESOME TENSES

The more common problems that are associated with verb tenses involve the various levels of present and past. Four levels exist and have traditional names:

| present | present perfect | past | past perfect |

For the purpose of sorting out the tenses here, however, the following names apply:

| present | connecting | past | past past |

Present. The present tense is used to report what is happening now:

> The employees *work* hard.

The present tense is also used to describe a universal truth: The earth *revolves* around the sun. This use of the present tense is called upon by writers to describe an object that always looks the same or a process that always works the same. The present tense is used in this manner even though the pertinent observations were obviously made in the past:

> While we *were* at the printing plant we saw how a mechanical binding *is* made. This type of binding *holds* together notebooks and other types of books that must open flat. To begin the process a machine *punches* round or slotted holes through the binding edges of the pages. Then the operator *inserts* coils or rings through the holes.

Present tense can also be used (and most often is) when writing about quotations. This use is known as the *historical present*. The historical present adds a feeling of immediacy to the quotation and is used in full view of the knowledge that the quote was written in the past:

> Thoreau *writes,* ''Simplify, simplify.''

Connecting (present perfect). The connecting tense is used to refer to an action that started in the past and is in some way connected to or continuing in the present. *Has* or *have* help form the connecting tense:

> Because the employees *have worked* so hard, the project is ahead of schedule. (The employees may still be working hard, for the project is still continuing.)

Past. Past tense is used to describe past actions that usually are connected with a definite time or set of conditions:

> The employees *worked* hard last week.

Past past (past perfect). The past past tense is used to show that something happened in the past but prior to other events in the past. *Had* helps form the past past tense.

After the employees *had finished* the project, they painted the office.

Shifting tenses. Shifting tenses is allowed when necessary:

While we *were* (past) at the printing plant we *saw* (past) how a mechanical binding *is* (present) made. This type of binding *holds* (present) together notebooks and other types of books that must open flat. After we *had observed* (past past) this operation, we *moved* (past) to the section where personnel *make* (present) edition bindings. The people to do this work *were hired* (past) last month, and they *have been* (connecting) learning the trade since then.

AGREEMENT

Agreement means to make nouns and verbs match in number. That is, if the noun is a plural form, its verb should also be plural; if the noun is a singular form, its verb should be singular:

This *company* (singular) *demonstrates* (singular) progress.

Organization *members* (plural) *show* (plural) their initiative.

The problem gets more complicated when several words intercede between noun and verb:

The *record* (singular) of the valuations and changes *is* (singular) kept.

Property (singular) acquired through donations and transfers, including 350 acres of land and several buildings, *is* (singular) not described in this report.

SENTENCES

SENTENCE CONTENT

A sentence is an expression of a thought or a feeling. In its simplest form, a sentence has two essential elements: a subject and a predicate. The subject is who or what you are writing about. The predicate is the part of the sentence that says something about the subject.

The above definition can be added to by restating the advice of Theodore M. Bernstein, who advocates that a sentence should contain no more than one idea. For many years Bernstein was an editor on *The New York Times* and a professor of journalism at the Columbia University School of Journalism. He also wrote several enjoyable books on the art of writing clearly and accurately.

Here is what Bernstein has to say about sentence content: "The one-idea-to-a-sentence dictum is designed . . . for those kinds of writing in which instant clarity and swift reading, which are other ways of saying quick comprehension, are dominant desiderata. Such kinds of writing include the newspaper article, the complex technical article, and the article about a specialized field designed to be read by those who are not familiar with that field."[2]

The one-idea-to-a-sentence advice is especially useful when applied to sentences like this:

The words are those of Roger W. Craig, Project Director for the Northern Regional Center, a federally funded, department-hosted project that does research for participating agencies in the north central states, a territory which includes Minnesota, North Dakota, South Dakota, Iowa, Wisconsin, and Michigan's Upper Peninsula.

That sentence could be broken up in this manner:

The words are those of Roger W. Craig, Project Director for the Northern Regional Center. The center is a federally funded, department-hosted project that does research for participating agencies in the north central states. This territory includes Minnesota, North Dakota, South Dakota, Iowa, Wisconsin, and Michigan's Upper Peninsula.

SIMPLE SENTENCES

We'll begin an explanation of simple sentences by restating part of the sentence definition that appeared a few paragraphs back. The part we need is this: In its simplest form, a sentence has two essential elements: a subject and a predicate. The subject is who or what you are writing about. The predicate is the part of the sentence that says something about the subject.

The following are simple sentences in the purest of forms:

1. Birds fly.
2. Birds fly south.
3. Birds were flying south.

The subject of each sentence is *birds*. In 1, the predicate is *fly;* in 2, *fly south;* and in 3, *were flying south*. The predicate can be identified because it says something about the subject. In addition, the predicate has a verb or a verb phrase. In 1 and 2, the verb is *fly;* in 3, the verb phrase is *were flying*.

The simple sentence can begin to get complicated when we use compound subjects. A compound subject is a subject made up of two or more things or people, as is shown by the use of italics in samples 4 and 5:

4. *Clerks* and *typists* sit all day.
5. *The rash of bicycle accidents* and *the increased severity of injuries attributed to such accidents* have led many observers to push for more stringent safety regulations.

Another type of simple sentence that sometimes causes problems is the simple sentence with a compound predicate. Here, two or more verbs appear in the predicate. This form is shown by the italicized words in 6 and 7.

6. They *went* to the party and *drank* all the wine.
7. We *must evaluate* the programs of the branch offices and *work* with these branches to develop and maintain effective programs.

It is with the compound predicate that the writer of the next sentence went astray:

8. Field representatives explain the program, and assist in conducting meetings.

Sentence 8 is still a simple sentence, and no comma is needed to separate the parts of the predicate. Such sentences should be written straight through and left unpunctuated until you reach the place for the period.

COMPOUND SENTENCES

The writer who added the comma to sentence 8 was close to writing a compound sentence. A compound sentence is two simple sentences joined by a comma and a conjunction. The most commonly used conjunctions are *and, but, or, for,* and *yet.*

A compound sentence may be used when you wish to express two ideas that are equal in importance, as in example 9:

9.   Simple: The road was rough. The car was bouncing.
   Compound: The road was rough, and the car was bouncing.

In compound form, sentence 8 could appear like this:

10. Field representatives explain the program, and these representatives assist in conducting meetings.

What has been added is a second subject, *these representatives.* Therefore, another way of defining a compound sentence is to say that it consists of the following: subject plus predicate plus comma plus conjunction plus subject plus predicate.

Here are some more guidelines for writing compound sentences. First, do not join unrelated items:

11. The road was rough, and I like baseball.

To add ideas use *and:*

12. The road was rough, and the car was bouncing.

To show contrast use *but:*

13. The road was smooth, but the car was bouncing. (A stronger contrast can be shown by using *yet.*)

To describe alternatives use *or:*

14. I will go to the store, or I will go to the show.

In a causal relationship use *for:*

15. I work here, for I need the money.

Some variations on the form of the compound sentence are shown below.

Three simple sentences can be combined into one compound sentence:

16. The room was small, but it was well lighted, and it was adequately ventilated.

A compound sentence can combine two simple questions:

17. Where are the blank forms, and where are the pens?

Another technique for combining closely related simple sentences is to use a semicolon, as in 18:

18. Jogging is good for us; we should do it more often.

This discussion of simple and compound sentences ends with a mention that in some sentences the subject is understood. Brackets are placed around understood subjects in the following two examples:

19. [You] Use the vocabulary that you are both familiar with.
20. [You] Go to the store, and [you] buy some milk.

If the bracketed subjects are removed, the sentences still make sense.

COMPLEX SENTENCES

Problems with the writing of complex sentences usually involve punctuating the dependent clauses. An understanding of proper punctuation can be helped by some definitions:

A complex sentence consists of at least one independent clause and at least one dependent clause. An independent clause is a simple sentence (subject + predicate) that can stand alone. A dependent clause is a group of words that cannot stand alone.

When the dependent clause comes before the independent clause, the two are separated by a comma, as in example 21 (here all sample dependent clauses are italicized):

21. *When we drove on the rutted road,* the car bounced like a cheap toy.

The dependent clause in 21 is an essential dependent clause and can be defined as follows:

An essential dependent clause contains information necessary to the meaning of the sentence.

When an essential dependent clause follows the independent clause, no separating comma is used.

22. The car bounced like a cheap toy *when we drove on the rutted road*.

In examples 21 and 22, the clause *when we drove on the rutted road* is essential, for it establishes the conditions under which the car bounced.

When an essential dependent clause occurs within a sentence, no separating commas are used:

23. Clerks *who work during break* are insane.

The underlined dependent clause is essential to the meaning of the sentence. If we were to take out the dependent clause, the sentence would read "Clerks are insane." That would say that *all* clerks are insane.

Punctuating an essential dependent clause. The only time that an essential dependent clause is set off from the rest of the sentence by a comma is when the essential dependent clause comes before the independent clause.

Punctuating a nonessential dependent clause. Wherever a nonessential dependent clause occurs, it is set off by a comma or commas. Another definition is:

> A nonessential dependent clause is a clause that can be removed from the sentence without changing the meaning of the sentence.

Some examples of sentences with nonessential dependent clauses are:

24. *If all goes well,* we hope to move by May.
25. We hope, *if all goes well,* to move by May.
26. We hope to move by May, *if all goes well.*
27. The time for the meeting is 2 p.m., *which is an hour later than originally planned.*
28. Our newest equipment, *which we purchased last month,* needs some adjustments.

In 28, the clause *which we purchased last month* is nonessential, because the equipment is already identified by the words *our newest.* This example can be rewritten to show an essential dependent clause:

29. The equipment *which we purchased last month* needs some adjustments.

Now the dependent clause is essential, because it identifies the equipment.

VISUAL SUMMARIES

Summaries of the sentence patterns discussed in this section are shown in Figures III-C1 and III-C2.

The most commonly used conjunctions are *and, but, for,* and *or.* Dictionaries also show as conjunctions *nor, so, while, yet,* and other words.

Simple and Compound Sentences

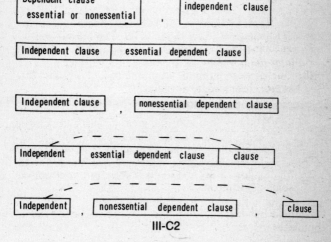

Simple: | Subject + predicate |

Compound: | Subject + predicate | , conjunction | subj. + pred. |

III-C1

Complex Sentences

| Dependent clause essential or nonessential | , | independent clause |

| Independent clause | | essential dependent clause |

| Independent clause | , | nonessential dependent clause |

| Independent | essential dependent clause | clause |

| Independent | , | nonessential dependent clause | , | clause |

III-C2

PUNCTUATING SENTENCE BEGINNINGS

A comma is often used after an introductory word, phrase, or clause that is separated by a slight pause from the rest of the sentence:

1. Nevertheless, the sprinkler system did not stop the fire.
2. Indeed, we did spend a lot of time on that project.

3. By the same token, the land should be theirs forever.
4. When we drove on the rutted road, the car bounced like a cheap toy.
5. In cases where the state has authority to and does transfer property that was granted for a specific purpose, the covenant continues to run with the land as long as the land is used for the granted purpose.

In some cases, the pause may not be abrupt enough to require a comma. Each of the following is acceptable:

6. In a recent letter, the manager told all personnel . . . .
7. In a recent letter the manager told all personnel . . . .

ORGANIZING ELEMENTS IN A SERIES

The organizing of sentence elements in a series sometimes poses problems. Which item should go first? Which, last? When can items be ranked in some kind of order? When is an alphabetical arrangement best? Answers to questions about series listings can be found in the following samples.

First, a series should be made up of similar elements. Villages, towns, and cities are similar elements. Villages, towns, and rivers are not similar elements.

Also, be sure to list series items in parallel form.

Wrong: We have three objectives in mind for the coming year: (1) increasing efficiency, (2) improve the quality of work, and (3) training new employees.
Better: . . . (1) increasing efficiency, (2) improv*ing* the quality of work, and (3) training new employees.

List events in the order in which they occur.

Wrong: We wish to evaluate, acquire, and publish new data.
Better: We wish to acquire, evaluate, and publish new data.

People are often listed by rank, most important person first, then descending in order. Another method, which will come close to achieving equality in the listing of people, is to list them alphabetically.

With regard to placing the most important item in a series,

two schools of thought exist. One school says that if you want to leave an impression on the reader or lead into the next sentence, place the important item last:

The fire caused almost $2 million in property damage, injured 65 persons, and killed 10 others.

The opposing view says to put the important item up front:

The fire killed 10 people, injured 65 others, and caused almost $2 million in property damage.

I'll leave it to you to be the judge of which sentence has the greatest impact.

PUNCTUATING ELEMENTS IN A SERIES

Elements in a series should be punctuated as follows:

The winter here is cold, wet, and windy.

Most newspapers and magazines would not call for the comma before the last item in a series. The opposite position is voiced by many writers of more formal and technical prose; these writers insist on using the last comma.

In the writing that we do in official letters, memos, and reports, we should use the comma before the last series element because:

- A comma is a mark of separation.

- If the last comma is omitted, the reader may be unable to answer the fundamental question: How many members are there in the series?

- Omission of the last comma almost always leads to confusion and sometimes guarantees it; including the last comma can never possibly confuse.

Consider: "red, brown, black and white dogs." Are the last dogs white only, or are they black and white? How can a reader tell? In short, use a comma before the last item in a series.

Correct examples of series punctuation are:

Because of the newness of the program, the stringency of the proposed standards, the increased demands on repair shops, and the limited supply of domes, the staff incorporated the new evaluation procedure.

and

This type of computer modeling requires data on temperature, altitude, wind speed, and aircraft gross weight.

If, however, you want to emphasize elements in a series, you can omit the commas and use only conjunctions:

The meeting dragged on for hours and hours and hours.

Another way to punctuate series items is with semicolons. This method is used when the items of the series are very long or contain internal punctuation, as in the following:

Conference participants represented the State of Arizona; Liquid and Bulk Tank Division, Fruehauf Corporation; Atlantic Richfield Company (ARCO); and the Phoenix Chamber of Commerce.

LOOSE AND PERIODIC SENTENCES

The immense popularity of scandal and gossip columns and magazines proves the axiom that people like stories about other people, conflict, and sex. Now there is virtually no way that we can make our official prose as juicy as even the most shopworn of scandals or so-called true confessions. But there are ways that we can put variety into our writing. One such way is to use different sentence types, such as the *loose* and the *periodic*.

Because loose and periodic sentences are opposites, it is easy to define and examine one against the other. In a loose sentence, the main elements come first and are followed by the modifying and explanatory items. In a periodic sentence, the modifying and explanatory items occur first, and the main meaning comes at the end. In a loose sentence, we turn loose of the main idea early. In a periodic sentence, we save the main idea until near the period. Some examples are:

Loose: The 747 landed early this morning, after a short flight from London.

Periodic: After a short flight from London, the 747 landed early this morning.

Loose: The new directive from the county board of

supervisors puts a freeze on all hiring until property tax rolls are straightened out and last year's
assessments are posted.

Periodic: Until property tax rolls are straightened out and
last year's assessments are posted, the new directive from the county board of supervisors
puts a freeze on all hiring.

The advantage of a loose sentence is that it is easy to construct. Still, it tends to trail off at the end. The advantage of a
periodic sentence is that in withholding information until the
end it can add suspense to writing. However, the periodic sentence can be much more difficult to read because the reader
may have to keep too much information suspended too long.

Loose sentences inform quickly. That's our goal, and our
writing should consist mainly of loose sentences. It is handy,
however, to know that the periodic sentence exists and can be
used occasionally to add variety to an otherwise dull report or
memo. And variety is needed, for without it our readers may
abandon us in favor of (you guessed it) stories about people,
conflict, and sex.

SENTENCE LENGTH

We can best get our ideas across if we use short sentences.
One reason concerns our ability to remember things. This is a
conclusion reached by George R. Klare, who has reviewed a
number of readability studies. Klare writes that ''Comprehension of written material depends upon the length of sentences
used, as readability studies show, probably because of human
limits in the memory span.''[3] In other words, by the time you
get to the end of a long sentence, you may have forgotten what
the beginning was all about.

A second reason to write short sentences relates to sentence
length versus comprehension. This relationship was the subject
of a study undertaken by the American Press Institute (API). In
its study the API tested college juniors and seniors on how well
they understood newspaper stories. The results were drawn up
as a chart that shows the relationship between reader comprehension and average sentence length. The chart is reprinted
here as Figure III-C3.

AMERICAN PRESS INSTITUTE READERSHIP SURVEY
READERS DEGREE OF UNDERSTANDING

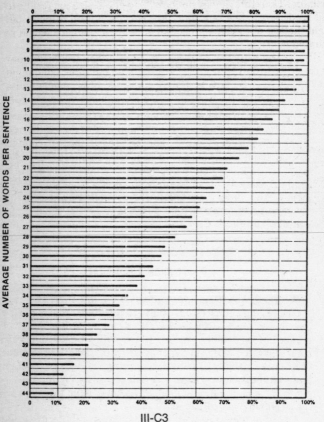

III-C3

This chart condenses the results of studies in comprehension made on 410 newspapers.

The studies correlated the average number of words in a sentence in stories with the reader's comprehension of those stories.

The studies revealed numerous cases in which the same word count resulted in the same percentage of comprehension. No attempt has been made here to indicate these duplications.

Please note that the API limited its test to college juniors and seniors. Therefore, it may not be safe to generalize the results to all readers. At the same time, however, it is safe to point out that the test does indicate the importance of sentence length to comprehension.

If you want to shorten the average sentence length of your writing, how do you do it? One way is to split long compound sentences in two by using a period instead of a comma and a conjunction. Another way is to make full sentences from subordinate clauses. You might also use an occasional sentence of from two to five words.

The comment must be made here that a short, poorly written sentence can contain more nonsense than a long, well-constructed one. It is also necessary to emphasize that the key word is *average*. That is, a mixture of sentence lengths adds variety to writing.

III-D.

PARAGRAPHS

A paragraph is made up of statements closely related to a single topic. When writing paragraphs, you should always plan them to serve the reader. You can do this by:

- Limiting a paragraph to statements that explain, describe, develop, or support one topic
- Announcing the topic early in the paragraph by using a topic sentence

Let's discuss these two concepts, beginning with the topic sentence.

Topic sentence. The topic sentence summarizes and introduces the central point of what the paragraph is all about. Our readers are best served if we make the first sentence the topic sentence, as in this example:

> The workload on our computer is more than it can handle. The overload is not enough to warrant buying an additional computer. However, we can rent some computer time from our sales office. We have explained the problem to the sales manager. He says it's okay with him.

The main idea—a problem with computer workload—is stated in the topic sentence that opens the paragraph. Supporting sentences give details on the solution.

For the reader, reading time is shortened. The reader will not have to dig into the paragraph to find out the paragraph's main point. Also, the reader can skim topic sentences to get the gist of your report and pick out the points that need additional investigation.

Unfortunately, writers do not always think in terms of topic sentences. Instead, we tend to develop ideas by first gathering them up in bits and pieces and then arriving at a conclusion. If we write a paragraph that way, the conclusion will find its way down to the bottom. In all likelihood, that conclusion is the topic sentence, and the topic sentence should be up at the top.

Therefore, what you may find yourself doing is writing the paragraph down in the order you thought it out and then rewriting it to serve the reader. To illustrate this point, let's assume that you are writing a lengthy report on the growth of the chemical industry. In the report, you have already established three characteristics of the industry and assigned them symbols: growth of capital investments (G_1), growth of major companies (G_2), and change in the number of companies in the industry (G_3). Now it becomes necessary to identify a fourth characteristic: rate of change of consumption of a substance (G_4). Your notes might begin like this:

NOTE VERSION

The chemical industry changes continually. Substances of concern today may be phased out, while the use of others may rise dramatically, thereby increasing their importance. For the purposes of this project, it therefore became necessary to calculate the rate of change of consumption of a substance. This rate was assigned the term G_4.

This paragraph does lead the reader into the definition of the new term, G_4. But remember that G_4 will be discussed partway into the report and that the purpose of the paragraph is to introduce G_4, not change in the chemical industry; the whole report is on such change.

Therefore, the sentence about G_4 is the topic sentence, and it should be moved from the bottom of the paragraph to the top. To do that, the entire paragraph is flip-flopped:

READER-ORIENTED VERSION

The term G_4 was assigned to mean the rate of change of consumption of a substance. It was necessary to calculate this rate because substances of concern today may be phased out, while the use of others may rise dramatically, thereby increasing their importance. This action is normal in the chemical industry, where change is continual.

Supporting the topic.   After the topic sentence, all other sentences give facts or concepts that will aid the reader's understanding of the topic. Notice how this is done in the following excerpt from Lewis Thomas' *The Lives of a Cell:*

> (1) Termites are even more extraordinary in the way they seem to accumulate intelligence as they gather together. (2) Two or three termites in a chamber will begin to pick up pellets and move them from place to place, but nothing comes of it; nothing is built. (3) As more join in, they seem to reach a critical mass, a quorum, and the thinking begins. (4) They place pellets atop pellets, then throw up columns and beautiful, curving, symmetrical arches, and the crystalline architecture of vaulted chambers is created. (5) It is not known how they communicate with each other, how the chains of termites building one column know when to turn toward the crew on the adjacent column, or how, when the time comes, they manage the flawless joining of the arches. (6) The stimuli that set them off at the outset, building collectively instead of shifting things about, may be pheromones released when they reach committee size. (7) They react as if alarmed. (8) They become agitated, excited, and then they begin working, like artists.[5]

Thomas begins by introducing the concept of termites accumulating intelligence in groups (Sentence 1). Within the paragraph, he announces two subtopics: thinking begins as more termites join together (Sentence 3), and it is not known how termites develop this collective intelligence (Sentence 5). The first subtopic is supported by the rich details Thomas provides in Sentence 4. The second subtopic is developed by description in Sentence 5 and the assumption made in Sentence 6. Sentences 2, 7, and 8 add further details and development.

Thomas supports his topic with seven sentences arranged into two subtopics. Other topics might need more support, while others can get by with far less.

Often there's no need to break a paragraph topic into subtopics. The following paragraph contains no subtopics and does not need as much development as Thomas' does.

> Before we can issue you an operator's license, you will have to clear a failure-to-appear notice that has been placed against your record. To do this, you must contact the Justice Court of your county. When corresponding with the court, refer to docket number 000000. The court will advise you of the amount of the fine.

Again, the main idea—the requirement to remove a failure-to-appear notice—is stated in the opening topic sentence. This is followed with three sentences of support that give specific instructions to the reader.

Paragraph length.   Any discussion of paragraph development and content leads automatically into the question of length. Generally speaking, longer, more formal pieces of writing such as reports are generally composed of longer paragraphs. Shorter works such as memos and letters are usually made up of shorter paragraphs. One-sentence paragraphs are acceptable, provided they adequately inform the reader. In fact, the trend today is toward shorter paragraphs just as it is toward shorter sentences.

A first step in monitoring paragraph length is to use the eye. That is, if a paragraph looks long and turns a page into a mass of gray, then look for a way to compose shorter paragraphs. Consider this marathon paragraph:

(1) The term G_4 was assigned to mean the rate of change of consumption of a substance. (2) It was necessary to calculate this rate because substances of concern today may be phased out, while the use of others may rise dramatically, thereby increasing their importance. (3) This action is normal in the chemical industry, where change is continual. (4) In evaluating the rate of change of consumption of a substance, two types of information sources were generally employed. (5) First, publications such as general reference works on industrial chemistry and chemical-specific studies, which are generally more up-to-date than the former, were examined for growth forecasts. (6) In most cases, these forecasts are on a nationwide basis. (7) Occasionally, clues are provided which enable one to evaluate potential growth in the state relative to the national forecasts. (8) Second, in our many telephone conversations with producer and user representatives, we gathered their views on national and, especially, statewide growth. (9) Our emphasis was therefore on contacting representatives who are intimately involved in the statewide market for each substance. (10) In this way, a reasonable estimate of the growth in the use of each substance was ascertained. (11) Nevertheless, such estimates are often relatively imprecise. (12) For this reason, broad ranges in growth rate were used in assigning values to G_4. (13) Also, when we were aware of developments which could most likely result

in a change in the growth rate, this information was factored into the choice of a value for G_4. (14) As an example, asbestos consumption is stable or is declining at quite a slow rate. (15) However, the pending phase-out of asbestos in many uses will hasten the decline in asbestos consumption, further encouraging the assignment of a value of 1 for G_4.

At a glance, that paragraph *looks* long. Then, a closer inspection shows that it contains material for three topics. The first topic introduces G_4; this topic begins at Sentence 1. The second topic describes the method used to evaluate G_4; this topic begins at Sentence 4. The third topic lists conditions attached to the value of G_4; this topic begins at Sentence 11. When that one long paragraph is broken into these three topics, the result is:

(1) The term G_4 was assigned to mean the rate of change of consumption of a substance. (2) It was necessary to calculate this rate because substances of concern today may be phased out, while the use of others may rise dramatically, thereby increasing their importance. (3) This action is normal in the chemical industry, where change is continual.

(4) In evaluating the rate of change of consumption of a substance, two types of information sources were generally employed. (5) First, publications such as general reference works on industrial chemistry and chemical-specific studies, which are generally more up-to-date than the former, were examined for growth forecasts. (6) In most cases, these forecasts are on a nationwide basis. (7) Occasionally, clues are provided which enable one to evaluate potential growth in the state relative to the national forecasts. (8) Second, in our many telephone conversations with producer and user representatives, we gathered their views on national and, especially, statewide growth. (9) Our emphasis was therefore on contacting representatives who are intimately involved in the statewide market for each substance. (10) In this way, a reasonable estimate of the growth in the use of each substance was ascertained.

(11) Nevertheless, such estimates are often relatively imprecise. (12) For this reason, broad ranges in growth rate were used in assigning values to G_4. (13) Also, when we were aware of developments which could most likely result in a change in the growth rate, this information was fac-

tored into the choice of a value for G_4. (14) As an example, asbestos consumption is stable or is declining at quite a slow rate. (15) However, the pending phase-out of asbestos in many uses will hasten the decline in asbestos consumption, further encouraging the assignment of a value of 1 for G_4.

The result is a page that has more eye appeal and that offers breaks in continuity that give readers a chance to take a breath.

Evaluating your paragraphs.   To evaluate your paragraphs, ask yourself these questions:

1. *Where* is the topic sentence?
2. Have I limited the paragraph to one main topic?
3. Have I thoroughly supported and developed this topic?
4. If the paragraph looks long, how can I break it into shorter paragraphs?

III-E.

COHERENCE:
TYING THOUGHTS TOGETHER

Coherence comes to writing when the thoughts hang together in print. Coherence is necessary because the reader's mind is different from the mind of the writer. Because of this difference, the reader may not see the same relationships as the writer. Therefore, it is the job of the writer to tie these relationships together.

TITLES AND HEADINGS

The way to start tying thoughts together is to announce what the thoughts are. Titles and headings do this.

Titles. A title should be as descriptive as possible without being as long as an abstract. In practice, a title is usually the result of a compromise between a statement that is short but not descriptive and a statement that is highly descriptive but too awkward to serve as a title.

As an example, consider this report's title: *The Gypsy Moth and Its Natural Enemies.*[6] Conceivably, the author might have simply used the title, *The Gypsy Moth.* That title leads the reader to believe that the report is a comprehensive document covering all aspects of the gypsy moth. On the other hand, a title such as *Patterns of Mortality-causing Factors that Operate against the Gypsy Moth Population* is too unwieldy. In this case, the title used was a wise compromise.

Titles are often written in full caps; that is, every letter is uppercased. An alternative is to initial cap the first word and every word except for articles, prepositions, and coordinating conjunctions. Articles are the words *a, an,* and *the.* The most commonly used prepositions are *at, by, for, from, in, of, on, to,* and *with.* The principal coordinating conjunctions are *and, but, for, nor,* and *or.*

Headings. Two different systems of report headings are shown here. Many variations are possible. Please note the use of capital letters, underlining, and indentation.

As much as possible, strive to make headings similar in sense and length. That is, avoid mixing a short, noun heading with a series of long heads dominated by verbs.

I. FIRST HEAD

A. SECOND HEAD
　　1. Third head.
　　　　a. Fourth head.

I.　FIRST HEAD
A. SECOND HEAD
　　1. Third head.
　　　　a. Fourth head.

III-E1

PARALLELISM

Parallelism in writing means "make the parts match." This doctrine of matching parts is based on the concept that ideas which are roughly alike in the writer's mind should look roughly alike in print. When the parts are not matched in print, the reader may wonder first about the writer's attention to detail and then about the writer's deeper thought processes. A brief guide to the doctrine of matching parts can be found by referring to the examples that follow.

Many problems with parallelism stem from the use of the wrong word:

Unmatched:　He was *ignorant* (adjective) and a *miser* (noun).

Matched:　He was *ignorant* (adjective) and *miserly* (adjective).

Unmatched:　*Preparation* of the solution, *heating* the

> beaker, and *pouring* the liquid. . . . (mixture of noun and verb forms)

Matched: *Preparing* the solution, *heating* the beaker, and *pouring* the liquid. . . .

A shift of point of view, like this change from personal to impersonal, can be distracting:

Unmatched: I shall first consider the advantages of the program, and second the disadvantages will be considered.

Matched: First I shall consider the advantages of the program, and second I shall consider the disadvantages.

Instructions are easiest to follow if given in matched forms:

Unmatched: First the nozzle should be placed in the fill pipe and next depress the lever.

Matched: First place the nozzle in the fill pipe and next depress the lever.

A shift in voice, such as this one from active to passive, is usually unnecessary:

Unmatched: We visited one field office, and selected hearings were analyzed.

Matched: We visited one field office, and we analyzed selected hearings.

or

We visited one field office and analyzed selected hearings.

One last point about parallelism can be made by looking back at the unmatched and matched examples. In almost all cases, matching the parts makes for brevity.

CONTINUITY AND TRANSITIONS

Reading is like traveling. You start, you journey through the pages, and you come to an ending point. If you are like most people, you prefer a smooth trip, as if you are being transported in the luxury of overstuffed velvet upholstery rather than being jolted over loosely set cobblestones. What makes this trip smooth for the reader is a form of pavement called continuity, and the writer can provide continuity by using transitions.

A transition may be a single word, a phrase, a sentence, a paragraph, or an even longer passage. You can use transitions to smooth out style, tell the reader what is coming next, or remind the reader about something that has happened earlier. In the paragraph above, I said that transitions can be used to provide a smooth journey through the pages. In the next paragraphs, we will see how transitions are used to develop a smooth style. We will also see how to set up patterns in the reader's mind that will carry him or her along with you. We will look at barriers to continuity, and we will examine a way to check how well transitions work.

Uses of transitional words and phrases.   A frequent use of transitions is to link sentences within a paragraph. This method can provide emphasis and make for smoother reading. In the following example, some standard transitional words and phrases smooth out what would otherwise be loosely set cobblestones:

> Each time a truck backs up to the loading ramp, it sounds its horn. *Unfortunately*, this practice has not reduced accidents. *Moreover*, the number of accidents is increasing, and this increase is wasting thousands of dollars in damage and nonproductive man-hours. *In addition*, the frequency of these accidents is demoralizing workers. *In fact*, the situation is so bad that many of the workers are threatening to go on strike.

Although the above sample probably uses too many transitions, it does show how they can be used.

Another way to smooth out writing is to repeat words and ideas, as in this sample:

> The politician's *promises* were so overstated that they drew only polite *applause*. As the *promises* became more exaggerated, the *applause* turned to silence. When an impossible *goal* was stated, many *people* began drifting away. On a final note of *hysteria*, the *crowd* broke up completely.

The italicized words in the above example establish patterns that repeat themselves in the reader's mind. Note also the use of the verbs *drew, turned, began drifting,* and *broke*. These verbs add movement to the pattern placed into the passage. The result is a paragraph that has continuity, but without the use of the more standard transitional words and phrases.

Whether you develop transitions by using the technique of repetition or by using standard transitional words and phrases, the result will be the same. Your writing will be smoother, and you will stand a better chance of carrying the reader along with you. You can then go one step farther toward keeping the reader on the road by using transitional sentences.

Transitional sentences. Transitional sentences can be used to link one paragraph to the next or to join sections of a manuscript. Two approaches to this problem are demonstrated in the following sample sentences:

> Having considered the more practical aspects of administering personnel performance tests just prior to quitting time, we now turn to the problem of employee fatigue at this time of day.

> or

> Even if administering personnel performance tests just prior to quitting time is a practical approach, there still remains the problem of employee fatigue at this time of day.

Either transition is good. The first is more direct; the second performs the function less obviously. The first might be easier to remember, but the second sample sounds smoother. The choice is up to the writer.

As a writer, you must also be aware that transitions introduce length into writing. For that reason, you should try to use the simplest transitional devices you can. Never use a paragraph when a sentence will do. Never use a sentence when a phrase will do. Never use a phrase when a word will do. Never use any transitional device if you don't need it. In short, don't overdo it.

SAMPLE TRANSITIONS

To introduce a topic.

additionally	a second point	likewise
again	further	moreover
also	furthermore	similarly
and	here	too
another	in addition	

To show that the same topic continues.

that	these	those
the same	this	

To restate a point.

in other words	that is to say	to put it differently

To concede a point.

granted	of course	to be sure

To present a contrast.

but	nevertheless	on the other hand
however	on the contrary	

As part of a cause and effect.

accordingly	consequently	therefore
as a result	for	thus
because	hence	

To point the reader in the right direction.

across the bay	here	in the southern
downwind from the site	there	part of the state

To guide the reader through time.

after several weeks	eventually	now
again	for the first time	since
and now	immediately	then
during all this time	later	ultimately
earlier	next	

To conclude.

all in all	finally	the point is
altogether	in conclusion	to summarize

BARRIERS TO CONTINUITY

Parenthetical barriers. One large barrier to continuity is caused by the writer who interrupts sentences by using long parenthetical elements (such as this one, which if it were truly parenthetical could be dropped from the sentence without being missed at all, but goes on and on and on) when they are not needed. If you must use parentheses to contain lengthy thoughts, try to write so that the parenthetical element will fall at the end of the sentence or paragraph.

Bunched-up nouns. Bunched-up nouns represent bunched-up thoughts. Readers find them hard to digest unless the thoughts are strung out and presented as bursts of information.

BUNCHED UP	STRUNG OUT
24-hour 100 micrograms per cubic meter state standard	state standard of 100 micrograms per cubic meter over 24 hours
state and local suspended emulsion particle standards	state and local standards for suspended emulsion particles
equal to or better collection efficiency than the nozzle tested	a collection efficiency that is equal to or better than the nozzle tested

Barriers and comprehension. Other barriers to continuity also obstruct comprehension. Long sentences that are packed with different ideas may confuse the reader and may require rereading before moving on. Commas and semicolons are marks of separation; too many of them are "brakes" on the forward movement of reading. Abstract terminology may make the reader stop and ask what it is you are trying to say. Unnecessary multisyllabic expressions make the reader work. In short, write lean and clean, simple and direct. That kind of style is easiest to understand and can be made to flow best.

THE SOUND OF PROSE

To check the smoothness of your writing, read it out loud. The mind's ear will hear what the eye does not see—and prose should sound good. Read your writing out loud to yourself, or have someone else read it to you. Read it into a tape recorder, and listen to the playback. Analyze what you hear. Be critical. The relationship between statements should be obvious. If a sentence sounds as if the paragraph is beginning again, the sentence probably needs attention. If it is difficult to pass from one idea to the next, the reader may be thrown off the track, and it is the writer's job to keep the reader on the track. That is what continuity is all about—keeping the reader on the track and giving the reader a smooth ride all the way to the end.

DETAILS: AN ALPHABETICALLY ARRANGED GUIDE TO CAPITALIZATION, NUMBERS, AND PUNCTUATION

APOSTROPHE

The apostrophe is used to show possession or omission, as in the following examples.

Possessive forms.   A singular or plural noun not ending in *s* is made into a possessive form by adding an apostrophe and an *s*:

man's, men's
Division's supply room

A singular noun ending in *s* or with an *s* sound is made into a plural by adding an apostrophe only (although an apostrophe and an *s* is encouraged by some style guides):

princess' (princess's) jewels
Schmitz' (Schmitz's) house

Plural possessives ending in *s* generally take only the apostrophe:

truck drivers' strike
businesses' employees

In compound nouns, the '*s* is added to the element nearest the item possessed:

comptroller general's decision
attorneys general's opinion

Combined possession is shown by placing an apostrophe in the last element:

soldiers and sailors' home
Sam and Joe's bar

Individual or alternative possession is shown by placing an apostrophe in each element:

men's, women's, and children's shoes
editor's or proofreader's opinion

Possessive indefinite or impersonal pronouns require an apostrophe:

each other's books   somebody's mistake
anyone's guess   somebody else's proposal

The possessive case is often used even though ownership is not involved:

30 days' notice   two hours' travel time
500 gallons' capacity   one day's work

Omission. An apostrophe is used in place of an omitted number or letter:

don't
spirit of '76
it's (*it is;* not *its* as a possessive)
o'clock (originally, *of the clock*)

Euphony. Tradition and the way words sound dictate the use of an apostrophe in cases like these:

for acquaintance' sake   for conscience' sake
for goodness' sake   for old times' sake

No apostrophe needed. Personal pronouns require no apostrophe:

theirs   hers
ours   its (not *it's* for *it is*)
his   whose (not *who's* for *who is*)

An apostrophe is not used in terms that are more descriptive than possessive:

United States control
technicians handbook
writers guide

Western States industries
teachers college

Coined plurals are normally written without an apostrophe:

the 1970s

B.A.'s and M.A.'s

but

49ers

I's and *we's*

ASTERISK

An asterisk (*) can be used to call attention to a footnote or to indicate omission. However, the asterisk is one of the most conspicuous of marks, and for that reason many writers use superior numbers for footnotes and three periods (four at the end of a sentence) to show omission.

BAR

The bar, slant, or virgule (/) is used in *and/or* or relationships like *feet/second*. The first use is often not necessary and may be avoided by just writing *or*. The second use should be restricted to mathematical forms or tables or graphs where space is at a premium.

BRACE

The brace is used to show the relation of one line or group of lines to another group of lines. The point of the brace is placed toward the fewer number of lines. If the number of lines is the same on each side of the brace, the point is placed toward the single title:

Intervals
of payment
$\left\{\begin{array}{l}\text{hourly}\\\text{daily}\\\text{weekly}\\\text{monthly}\end{array}\right.$

Pacific	⎰	California
Coast	⎱	Oregon
States		Washington

BRACKETS

Brackets are used in pairs to set off matter inserted by a writer into an original quotation. Such an insertion is meant to indicate a correction, explanation, omission, editorial comment, or a caution that an error is reproduced literally:

Our conference [lasted] two hours.
The general [Washington] ordered him to leave.
Our party will always serve the people [applause] in spite of the opposition [loud applause].
The statue [sic] was on the statute books.

CAPITALIZATION

No one needs to be told that sentences and proper nouns begin with capital letters. But what does a writer do about the vast majority of words where choice is allowed? Just be aware that capital letters call attention to writing, and that the trend today is toward the use of fewer capitals. Therefore, when in doubt, lowercase. And most important, be consistent, which is of course the best rule to follow in all your writing.

COLON

The colon is a mark of expectation. It tells the reader, "Watch what's coming":

My goal at work is simple: survival.

The following rule accompanies use of the colon:

Capitalize the first letter of a complete sentence that is introduced by a colon.

A colon is used in:

Salutations (Ladies and Gentlemen:)
Clock time (2:40 p.m.)

A colon is also used before long or formal quotations:

Education Code Section 00000 states: "The Legislature finds and declares. . . ."

COMMA

Some standard uses of the comma are shown in the following examples.

In numbers of four or more, to separate thousands, millions, and the like:

4,320   1,150,000

Note: This rule does not apply to a number containing four or more digits as used in serial numbers, street addresses, telephone numbers, page numbers, radio frequencies, and military time.

In full dates:

They left on January 2, 1976, for Los Angeles.

But not in partial dates:

They left in January 1976 for Los Angeles.

With places and forms of address:

The meeting took place in Eugene, Oregon, last month.
Texaco, Inc., refinery
Washington, D.C., offices
John Smith, Jr., and Alfred E. Jones, Ph.D., work here.

To introduce a short, direct question:

At this point we must ask, What can be done now?

Around words or phrases that interrupt:

There are, of course, other reasons.
We must remember, however, that no guarantee is attached.

To set off items in apposition or in contrast:

Mr. Green, the lawyer, spoke for industry.
The word ends with an *s,* not a *z.*

To indicate omission:

Then we had much; now, nothing.
Chief, Department of Finance

With quotation marks:

He said, "Write that letter."
"I will," she answered, "if you will help me."

Exception: A long or formal quotation is introduced with a colon.

To separate numbers for clarity:

In 1975, 431 applicants took the test.

To separate coordinate adjectives:

The large, cold house.
The shrewd, scheming politician.

Exception: A comma is not used when the adjectives are not coordinate:

A heavy steel pipe
An old porcelain tub

Note: Noncoordinate adjectives can be spotted in two ways. First, if you insert an *and* between them the result sounds awkward: a heavy and steel pipe. Second, if you reverse the adjectives the result is again awkward: a steel heavy pipe.

For other uses of the comma, see chapter III-C on sentences.

DASH

The dash is made on the typewriter by using two hyphens (--) that are not spaced away from the surrounding words. The dash is a bold horizontal mark in a thicket of type in which the letters are formed by essentially vertical strokes. This contrast makes the dash an emphatic device. This emphasis can be made the most of if used sparingly.

The dash can be used to make interrupting elements stand out:

The system failed testing—it was the fourth failure in a row—for the same reasons as before.

The dash can be used to emphasize the final idea in a sentence:

> He smiled and asked how she liked her job, whether she liked her new boss, how she felt, and what her plans were—but he didn't care at all.

The dash can also be used to show interruption in dialogue or testimony:

> "Such an idea can scarcely be—"
> Q. Did you see—
> A. No, sir.

EXCLAMATION MARK

The exclamation mark is seldom, if ever, used in business and technical writing.

HYPHEN

Most problems involving hyphens can be resolved by applying the following general principles.

A good starting point is a dictionary. For a word in common usage, a dictionary will often show if the word is hyphenated, written as a solid compound (such as *roughshod*), or formed as an open compound (as an example, *round lot*). A dictionary is also helpful for questions concerning hyphens in the following forms: figures of speech; prefix combinations (involving, as examples, *anti, co, extra, intra, mis, multi, non, post, pre, pro, sub, super,* and *un*); fractions, numerals, and mathematical compounds in popular use; more generally known scientific and technical terms; and so-called improvised compounds (such as *know-it-all* and *H-bomb*).

If a dictionary does not show a hyphenated form of the word in question, then follow this general guide: When a temporary compound is used as an adjective before a noun, the temporary compound is often hyphenated to avoid misleading the reader. As an example, without a hyphen in *common-noun title,* the reference may be to a noun title that is common.

However, if you place this same type of modifier after a noun, the relationship is sufficiently clear, and the compound is left open: *title* containing a *common noun.*

A hyphen is also used to prevent ambiguity in compounds

such as *un-ionized* (as compared to *unionized*) and *pre-position* (as compared to *preposition*).

Some compound forms are hyphenated (and sometimes called *improvised compounds*) regardless of where they fall in a sentence. Examples of these are *bull's-eye* and *penny-wise*.

Not hyphenated are *ly* compounds such as *wholly owned subsidiary* and *eagerly awaited moment*.

Suspensive hyphens are shown in this sentence: "The staff predicts there will be no long- or short-term adverse impact," which can also be written as "long-term or short-term."

Some other points are: For scientific terms that are new or in limited use, follow the practice of the profession concerned. For guidance in splitting words at the end of a line, consult a dictionary.

NUMBERS

Your reader understands numerals more readily than words used for numbers. This is especially true in technical material. For example, *87* is clearer than *eighty-seven*. Therefore, the following are almost always written as numerals: addresses, ages of people, chapters, clock hours (especially when the exact moment is to be emphasized), dates, decimals, distances, fractions, game scores, illustrations, mathematics, measurements, money, pages, pressures, statistics, telephone numbers, and volumes.

There are instances, though, when numbers should be spelled out. These instances are shown here.

The basic rule.   For a single number, spell out if under 10, and use numerals for 10 and over:

Our district has three elementary schools.
The neighboring district has 12 elementary schools.

For two or more numbers in the same sentence, spell them out if all are nine or under; if any number is over nine, use numerals for all:

Our district has three elementary schools, and the neighboring district has five.

but

Our district has 3 elementary schools, but the neighboring district has 12.

Note: More formal writing styles substitute *100* for *10* in this rule.

Initial numbers. At the beginning of a sentence, spell out any number that would otherwise be written as a numeral:

Eighty-nine pupils attend one school.

If spelling out a number at the beginning of a sentence looks awkward, recast the sentence so that it does not begin with a number:

One school has 89 pupils.

Dialogue or narrative text. In prose narrative or dialogue, the appearance of the page sometimes dictates that numbers be spelled out regardless of size:

They always go to bed at eleven.
Be in your room by half-past nine.

Mixed numbers. To avoid the confusion that might arise from writing 3 4-foot poles, mixed numbers are written like these:

three 4-foot poles
eleven ¼-inch lines

but

120 8-inch boards

Numbers in titles of organizations.

Ninety-third Congress   First Baptist Church
Tenth Circuit Court   Fourteenth Precinct

but

Union Local No. 16

Certain fractions. Fractions standing alone or followed by the words *of a* or *of an* are usually spelled out:

one-third-inch-thick plate
one-quarter of a mile from the junction

Indefinite, large, and round numbers.

several thousand people
the early seventies
a two-thousand-word report
2.3 billion instead of 2,300,000,000
$1 million instead of $1,000,000

General cautions.

1. Arabic numbers are easier to read than roman.
2. If you use roman numerals, don't use the symbol MM to stand for a million. This usage has come into vogue in the past few years and is based on the premise that a thousand times a thousand (M times M) equals a million. However, roman symbols add or subtract; they do not multiply. Hence, MM Btu is not a million British thermal units; it is 2,000 Btu. The correct roman symbol for a million is $\overline{\text{M}}$. Of course, you could write M for *mega* or use 10^6. But, as always, you can't go wrong if you spell out.
3. Don't mix metric and English units unless you give the reader a conversion key.

PARENTHESES

Parentheses can be used in place of commas or dashes to set off parenthetical ideas. Parenthetical ideas generally occur in one of three categories: (1) those ideas that are closely related in thought and structure to the rest of the sentence; (2) those ideas that forcefully or abruptly interrupt the rest of the sentence; and (3) those ideas that are more remote in thought and structure from the rest of the sentence. The following sentences illustrate this tendency:

The system failed testing, which was conducted according to less stringent standards, for the same reasons as before.

The system failed testing—it was the fourth failure in a row—for the same reasons as before.

The system failed testing (We had contacted the manager before starting.) for the same reasons as before.

Parentheses and remotely related parenthetical comments should be used sparingly. Their use interrupts the flow of information to the reader and slows down communication. If the ideas in the last sample above really were related, the sentence would have read more smoothly this way: "Although we had contacted the manager before starting testing, the system failed for the same reasons as before."

The use of other punctuation marks with parentheses sometimes poses problems. A guideline is: When the parenthetical unit is a complete sentence, the end punctuation is placed *inside* the parentheses. Other correct punctuation combinations are:

". . . has taken over that role" (*U.S. News & World Report,* December 19, 1977, p. 11).

". . . has taken over that role." (See *U.S. News & World Report,* December 19, 1977, p. 11.)

Parentheses are also used to number lists, such as (1), (2), and (3) or 1), 2), and 3); and to introduce abbreviations: Internal Investigation and Control Division (IICD)

PERCENT OR %?

In technical and scientific writing styles use %. In prose styles characteristic of the social sciences and the humanities, use *percent* (one word).

PERIOD (INCLUDING ELLIPSIS POINTS)

Periods are used to end sentences that do not ask direct questions or do not make exclamations. Periods are also used with certain abbreviations and as ellipsis points to show that the writer has left something out of quoted material. The first use seldom causes problems. Guidance for the second use is best obtained from a dictionary. It is with the third use, periods as ellipsis points, that we are concerned here.

Ellipsis points are typed as three periods with a space between each period, a space before the first period, and a space after the third period (. . .). The three ellipsis points indicate an omission from a quoted sentence. Other punctuation may be used on either side of the three ellipsis points if the other punctuation helps the sense of the quotation, better shows what has been omitted, or is necessary to maintain the integrity of a quotation.

Four dots—a period followed by three ellipsis points—indicate the omission of (1) the last part of quoted sentence, (2) the first part of the next sentence, (3) a whole sentence or more, or (4) a whole paragraph or more. When the original sentence ends with a question mark or an exclamation mark, this mark is kept in favor of the period, and three points are used to show the ellipsis.

The uses of ellipsis points are demonstrated in the following passages:

> In their operational planning activities, trucking companies use computers to plan daily pickup and delivery routes. Among the complicating factors that must be considered are (1) the large number of pickup and delivery points, (2) warehouse locations, (3) frequency of daily pickups and deliveries, and (4) types of trucks available. In addition to planning and scheduling truck movements to give good service and maximize the consolidation of freight hauled by each unit, trucking firms have also used simulation techniques to evaluate the effects of changes in routes, demand for services, number and/or location of warehouses, and changes in equipment.

becomes

> In their . . . activities, trucking companies use computers to plan daily pickup and delivery routes. . . . In addition to planning and scheduling truck movements to give good service and maximize the consolidation of freight hauled by each unit, trucking firms have also used simulation techniques to evaluate the effects of changes in routes, demand for services, number and/or location of warehouses, and changes in equipment.

or

> In their . . . activities, trucking companies use computers to plan daily pickup and delivery routes. . . . In addition to planning and scheduling truck movements . . . , trucking firms have also used simulation techniques to evaluate the effects of changes in routes, demand for services, number and/or location of warehouses, and changes in equipment.[7]

QUESTION MARK

A question mark is used at the end of a direct question, but not an indirect one:

Direct: What is the real reason?
Indirect: It would help to know the real reason.

QUOTATION MARKS AND QUOTATIONS

General rules.   Some general rules for quoting from the speech or writing of another are:

- The source's wording, spelling, punctuation, and capitalization must be copied faithfully.

- The initial letter and final punctuation of a quotation may be changed to make the quotation fit the style and structure of the text.

- An explanation, correction, or comment may be put in brackets and inserted into the quotation.

- When proofreading and rechecking quotations, the final typed draft must be compared against the original source or a photocopy of the original source, not intervening drafts.

Form: run in or indented.   A quotation may be incorporated directly into the text (run in) or indented in block form. Block form is usually reserved for quotations of 8 to 10 lines or longer. However, if quotations are to be compared, the writer should use block form even for quotations of only one or two lines.

Use of the marks.   American practice generally follows the double-single-double pattern of using quotation marks. That is, double quotation marks enclose words, phrases, and sentences that are run into the text, single quotation marks enclose quotations inside double marks, double inside of single, and so on. Whenever possible, the writer should limit the use of the marks to two or at the most three sets. To do otherwise is to ask the reader to keep track of too much at one time:

He told us, "The reporter says 'the Senator answered "no" to charges that he had been taking bribes.' "

If quotation marks are needed inside of block quotations, the same pattern applies: double first, single inside double, even if the source used the marks in the opposite pattern. Block quotations themselves are not set off with quotation marks. When a quotation is carried through more than one paragraph, each paragraph has quotation marks at the start, but closing quotation marks are not used until the quotation ends.

Introducing quotations.   When introducing quotations, punctuation and capitalization are determined by how smoothly the writer works the quotation into the text. The following illustrations show different techniques:

> Mrs. Malaprop mistakenly informs us that ''he is the very pineapple of politeness.''

or

> Mrs. Malaprop mistakently informs us that ''He is the very pineapple of politeness.''

or

> According to Mrs. Malaprop, ''He is the very pineapple of politeness.''

or

> Mrs. Malaprop says the following: ''He is the very pineapple of politeness.''

If Mrs. Malaprop's words are to be written as testimony, quotation marks are not needed:

> Mrs. Malaprop: He is the very pineapple of politeness.

End punctuation.   End punctuation with quotation marks follows these general guides:

- The comma and the period are placed inside the quotation marks.
- The colon and the semicolon are placed outside the quotation marks.
- The dash, exclamation mark, and question mark are placed outside the quotation marks unless part of the quotation.

Some examples are:

> He asked, ''Will you write that letter?''
> ''Will you write that letter?'' he asked.
> ''Write that letter,'' he said.
> ''I will,'' she answered, ''if you will help.''
> What is meant by an ''eye for an eye''?
> A shout—''Help!''—broke the silence.

As the door slammed, she yelled, "Let me ex—"
Read the editorial "Haphazard Budgeting"; it will disgust
you.

If a quotation is followed by parenthetical documentation, the
end punctuation is placed after the parentheses:

". . . has taken over that role" (*U.S. News & World Report*, December 19, 1977, p. 11).

but

". . . three full days at the wheel!" (*Road & Track*, January 1978, p. 46).

A footnote reference goes outside the quotation marks:

The exact words are: "The facts prove otherwise."[2]

Additional uses. An additional use of quotation marks is to
enclose titles of songs, short poems, and works that are parts of
a larger work, such as articles as part of a magazine, chapters of
a book, and sections of a report. The title of the larger work is
underlined (or set in italic type if printed).

Also, quotation marks can be used to call attention to an
unusual word or a word used in an unusual way. This use should
be kept to a minimum, however. Quotation marks call attention
to a page, and too many of them give a page a cluttered look.
Any tendency to overuse quotation marks in this regard can be
reduced if the writer will keep in mind the primary purpose of
the marks: to show what has been taken directly from the
speech or writing of another.

Dialogue. Dialogue is enclosed in quotation marks. A
change of speaker is usually indicated by a new paragraph.

"What time does the party start?"
"Not for another two hours, I was told. But the way some
people look, it's started already."

Exceptions. Quotation marks are not used with *yes* or *no*
except in dialogue.

The answer is no, although it should have been yes.
"No," he answered.

When quoting from legal documents, any change in capitalization is indicated by brackets:

"[t]he state board is designated"
"[P]ursuant to Chapter 2"

Also, if precision when quoting from legal works is desired, punctuation that is not part of the quotation is placed outside the quotation marks:

"water quality standards".

SEMICOLON

The semicolon suffers from an identity crisis, for it is not half a colon as *semi* implies. Neither is a semicolon used to introduce, the way a colon is, or even to half introduce. For purposes of definition, it might be best to think of the semicolon as half a period, for the semicolon is truly a mark of separation, and its use falls somewhere between a period and a comma.

As half a period, the semicolon can be used in constructions like these:

It is true in peace; it is true in war.

instead of

It is true in peace. It is true in war.

They priced the car low; therefore, it sold on the first day.

instead of

They priced the car low. Therefore, it sold on the first day.

The semicolon can be used to separate series elements that contain commas:

They lived in Seattle, Washington; Portland, Oregon; and Las Vegas, Nevada.

UNDERLINING (ITALICS)

Underlining is used in typewritten copy to correspond with the use of italic type in printed forms (except most newspapers and some magazines). The uses of underlining are:

To introduce a key term. The term is not underlined in later uses:

It is convenient to introduce the concept of *pressure*. Pressure is defined as. . . .

In titles of legal cases, with the names of plaintiff and defendant:

Miranda v. *Arizona*

When writing about letters as letters and words as words:

The last letter is an *s*, not a *z*.
It is not half a colon as *semi* implies.

With the name of a specific ship, submarine, aircraft, or spacecraft. The preceding abbreviation is not underlined:

USS *Nautilus*
but Boeing 727 (type of plane)

With the title of a book, periodical, newspaper, or similar publication:

Los Angeles Times
The Serial: A Year in the Life of Marin County
Harrison County Irrigation District Rules and Regulations
Road & Track

Note: Long titles are extra work for writer, typist, and reader. Therefore, after the first full citation, use short titles or references. The samples below show such techniques:

In *The Serial: A Year in the Life of Marin County*, "Staying Mellow in Marin" is the title of the first chapter. . . . A confusing point in *The Serial* occurs when. . . . Then too, the characters in Cyra McFadden's *Serial* are. . . . In sum, the book represents only one author's view of modern life.

In the *Harrison County Irrigation District Rules and Regulations*, "Users' Rights" is the title of Regulation III. . . . Then too, the language in the *Rules and Regulations* leads one to. . . . A later point in the Harrison County Irrigation District's *Rules and Regulations* is. . . . Final opinion on these rules and regulations rests in the hands of the user.

Underlining is also used with genus and species, unfamiliar foreign words and phrases (check a dictionary), titles of plays, paintings, motion pictures, television and radio programs, and titles of long poems and long musical works.

Not underlined are the plural parts of underlined singulars:

The newsstand was out of *Chronicle*s and *Examiner*s.

Underlining (italics) can be used to add emphasis, but this is mechanical or forced emphasis and is showy. For that reason, underlining for emphasis is rarely done in any kind of writing and is almost universally verboten in technical writing.

If you use underlining to call attention to a point in a quotation, tell the reader. If the emphasis is part of the original, again let the reader know. The techniques are:

"*All* artists argue about their ways of performing" [emphasis added].

"Use the book like a person to listen to and *argue with*" [Barzun's emphasis] or [emphasis in original].

IV.

EDITING YOUR WRITING

Blot out, correct, insert, refine,
Enlarge, diminish, interline.
Jonathan Swift ("On Poetry")

IV.

EDITING YOUR WRITING

Readers see your publications as part of your organization's programs and thinking. Readers are impressed by quality work.

Your organization's image can be hurt, however, by typographical errors, misspelled words, faulty grammar, long and disorganized documents, pages missing or out of sequence, and a host of other faults, minor and major.

Close attention to detail while writing will prevent most of these mistakes. Careful editing will find and correct the rest.

Accordingly, the material presented here is planned to lead you through the editing process, beginning with simple editing exercises and ending with a discussion of the very difficult task of editing the writing of another.

EDITING EXERCISES

Editing exercise #1. Let's take the following passage, which is the preface to the *U. S. Government Printing Office Style Manual,* and edit it. Overall, the preface is well written and will serve as a relatively easy introduction to editing. While working on the preface, our goal is to retain the original meaning and style while shortening it wherever possible and striving to improve clarity. Here is the preface in full:

PREFACE

Line
number
1. By act of Congress the Public Printer is
2. authorized to determine the form and style of

3. Government printing. The Style Manual is the
4. product of many years of public printing
5. experience, and its rules are based on
6. principles of good usage and custom in the
7. printing trade. In addition, the Manual
8. attempts to keep abreast of and sometimes
9. anticipate changes in orthography, grammar, and
10. type production. It has grown with Government
11. and the ever-expanding body of language with
12. new terms and expressions.

13. Essentially, it is a standardization device
14. designed to achieve uniform word and type
15. treatment, and aiming for economy of word use.
16. Such rules as are laid down for the submission
17. of copy to the GPO point to the most economical
18. manner for the preparation and typesetting of
19. manuscript. Following such rules eliminates
20. the need of additional chargeable processing by
21. the GPO.

22. It should be remembered that the Manual is
23. primarily a GPO printers stylebook. Easy rules
24. of grammar cannot be prescribed, for it is
25. assumed that editors are versed in correct
26. expression. As a printers book, it necessarily
27. uses terms which are obvious to those skilled in
28. the graphic arts. A glossary of such printing
29. terms to be complete would unnecessarily burden
30. the Manual. (See bibliography on pp. 2-3.)

31. Its rules cannot be regarded as rigid, for the
32. printed word assumes many shapes and variations
33. in type presentation. An effort has been made
34. to provide complete coverage of those elements
35. which enter into the translation of manuscript
36. into type.

37. For the purposes of this Manual, printed
38. examples throughout are to be considered the
39. same as the printed rules.[1]

Let's edit for brevity first.

First paragraph

2. Delete *form and*. The word *style* is inclusive enough to convey the intended meaning.

4. Delete *many* and *public printing*. *Many* is a vague word that adds nothing solid to this sentence. As for *public printing*, what other kind of experience would the Public Printer have?

6. Delete *principles of* as being unnecessary.

**11.
and
12.** Delete *with new terms and expressions;* these words are included in the definition of *ever-expanding body of language*, on line 11.

Second paragraph

13. Replace *Essentially, it is a standardization device* with *The Manual is*. The word *standardization* is not needed, for its thought is repeated in *uniform* (line 14).

15. Delete *aiming for;* the comma before *and* is also unnecessary.

16. Delete *Such* and *as are laid down*. These words add nothing to the sentence.

20. Delete *the need of;* these three words are unnecessary. Change *chargeable processing* to *charges*.

Third paragraph

23. Delete *Easy;* it adds nothing to the sentence and implies that hard rules of grammar can be prescribed.

26. Delete *necessarily;* this thought is expressed in the words *As a printers book* (line 26).

**28.
and
29.** Delete *printing;* the reader has the point by now that this is a printers book. Place *complete* in front of *glossary* and delete *to be;* these changes tighten up the sentence. Delete *unnecessarily*. Would a glossary *necessarily* be a burden?

Last two paragraphs

31. Change *cannot be regarded as* to *are not*.

33. Delete *in type presentation*. How else can the printed word (line 32) be presented?

34.   Change *provide complete coverage of* to *completely cover*.

37.   Change *For the purposes of* to *In*. Delete *printed* and
and   *throughout*.
38.

39.   Delete *printed*.

What needs to be done now is to correct two minor problems of clarity.

Paragraph number	*Correction*
1	Change *orthography* to *spelling*.
1, 2, and 3	Some readers may be confused by the mixture of the terms *Public Printer* and *GPO*, the latter being an undefined abbreviation for Government Printing Office, which is the same as the Public Printer. This confusion can be prevented by using only one term (GPO) and by defining it the first time it appears, in the first sentence: "By act of Congress the Government Printing Office (GPO) is authorized. . . ."

The preface now looks like this:

By act of Congress the Government Printing Office (GPO) is authorized to determine the style of Government printing. The Style Manual is the product of years of experience, and its rules are based on good usage and custom in the printing trade. In addition, the Manual attempts to keep abreast of and sometimes anticipate changes in spelling, grammar, and type production. It has grown with Government and the ever-expanding body of language.

The Manual is designed to achieve uniform word and type treatment and economy of word use. Rules for the submission of copy to the GPO point to the most economical manner for the preparation and typesetting of manuscript. Following such rules eliminates additional charges by the GPO.

It should be remembered that the Manual is primarily a GPO printers stylebook. Rules of grammar cannot be prescribed, for it is assumed that editors are versed in correct expression. As a printers book, it uses terms which are obvious to those skilled in the graphic arts. A complete glossary of such terms would burden the Manual. (See bibliography on pp. 2-3.)

Its rules are not rigid, for the printed word assumes many shapes and variations. An effort has been made to completely cover those elements which enter into the translation of manuscript into type.

In this Manual, examples are to be considered the same as the rules.

The editorial changes made to the *Style Manual*'s preface were minor in that only a small percentage of the words were deleted or changed. The lesson to be learned from this type of exercise is that much of editing—and writing—consists of a constant effort to find and eliminate the unnecessary word, no matter how small. In this case, the result is a rewritten preface that is 12 lines shorter than the original version.

Editing exercise#2. The preface just edited had insignificant problems compared to the following example. Only one sentence long, it screams to be shortened.

Lastly, in a further, more general principle, overall the concentration of this document is saying that both uniformity and diversity need to be included in a healthy tandem, or tension, or relationship to each other and that the areas, where uniformity might be needed, must respect the possibility of more flexibility within a school and the areas, where obviously there could be more diversity, must remember that certain areas necessitate a more uniform and standard approach.

Reread that long-winded monster, and note these repeated terms: "uniformity," "diversity," "uniformity," "flexibility," "diversity," and "uniform." Note that (1) these terms are used with respect to a school, (2) that the sentence refers to a "healthy tandem, or tension, or relationship," and that (3) the sentence begins by speaking of "lastly" and "overall."

When you put all these principal words together, you can write the same thing in these few words:

In summary, a proper balance of uniformity and diversity must be maintained within a school.

If you ever have to edit anything like that, you will have to be ruthless. Search for the main ideas, and cut them down to as few words as possible.

AN EDITING CHECKLIST

The following short checklist is meant to serve as a guide for reviewing the final product.

1. Titles and headings
   a. Is the title of the publication adequate and correct?
   b. Is the title page arranged correctly?
   c. Are chapter titles parallel in structure?
   d. Are section titles parallel in structure?
   e. Are headings parallel in structure?
   f. Are the subheads parallel in structure?
2. Text
   a. Does the text read smoothly?
   b. Is each sentence complete?
   c. Is each paragraph complete?
   d. Is each section complete?
   e. Is each chapter complete?
   f. Are chapters parallel in structure?
   g. Is punctuation correct?
   h. Is capitalization consistent?
   i. Are arguments, ideas, and relationships thoroughly developed?
   j. Is each visual aid introduced correctly?
   k. Is each appendix introduced correctly?
   l. Are all footnotes complete?
   m. Are all footnotes in correct form?
   n. Are names of persons and organizations correct?
3. Visual aids
   a. Is the title of each visual aid correct?
   b. Are the titles of the aids uniform?
   c. Are the titles of the aids parallel?
   d. Are the aids numbered in the correct sequence?
   e. Is each part of each aid titled correctly?
   f. Is each aid documented correctly?
   g. Is each aid aligned correctly on the page?
   h. Are tables ruled correctly?
   i. Is each aid related to the text?
   j. Is any aid cluttered or "busy"?
4. Quoted and cited material

    a. Is each quotation accurate?
    b. Is each quotation documented correctly?
    c. Is each legal statement accurate?
    d. Is each legal statement documented correctly?
    e. Have necessary permissions to quote been received?

5. Mathematics and statistics
    a. Are all statistics accurate?
    b. Do the parts and totals of statistics balance?
    c. Is the source of each statement of statistics shown correctly?
    d. Is the math accurate?
    e. Have mathematical symbols been replaced with plain English in the text wherever possible?

6. Back matter
    a. Is the bibliography adequate?
    b. Is each entry in the bibliography in correct form?
    c. Is each appendix necessary?
    d. Are the appendixes in the right order?
    e. Is the index adequate and accurate?

7. Table of contents
    a. Is the table of contents complete?
    b. Are page numbers correct?

8. Physical appearance
    a. Is there too much clutter?
    b. Is any paragraph a mass of gray?
    c. Is the type too faint?
    d. Are all parts of the manuscript present and in the right order?
    e. Are all pages present?

EDITING MARKS; PROOFREADING TIPS

Editing marks.   Editing marks such as those shown in Figure IV-1 are used when correcting drafts.

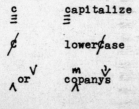

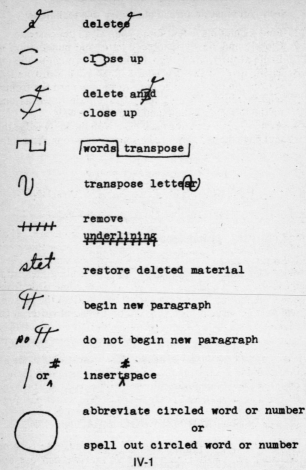

ⅆ	delete
⌒	close up
ⅆ⃥	delete and close up
⌐⌐	words transpose
∿	transpose lette(er)
+++++	remove underlining
stet	restore deleted material
⁋	begin new paragraph
No ⁋	do not begin new paragraph
/ or ∧	insert space
◯	abbreviate circled word or number or spell out circled word or number

IV-1

Proofreading tips. The best way to proofread is to work with another person called the copyholder. The copyholder reads out loud from the manuscript, enunciates clearly, and announces punctuation marks. The author or editor follows along on the final typed copy or the printer's proofs. This method is expensive, for it ties up two people. What often results then is a lot of solitary proofreading, which is very hard to do.

So if you must proofread alone, try this technique.

1. Find a quiet place and force yourself to concentrate.
2. Closely and slowly read each letter and punctuation mark. Begin at the front and go all the way through to the end.
3. Then, reverse the procedure. Read each word and mark, starting on the last page and working toward the front. You might even try turning the pages upside down as another method of seeing the manuscript a new way.
4. As a last resort, attack each page with the knowledge that on that page there just has to be something wrong. You'll find it.

EDITING SOMEONE ELSE'S WRITING

This section of the book is written with the thought that some day you will have to edit the writing of someone else. The time may come when a co-worker asks you to "look this over and tell me what you think of it." When you become a supervisor, much of your time will be taken up with editing the writing of those who work for you. Or you may become a professional editor. Although the material here is planned for the person who will have to serve primarily as editor instead of writer, it can be relied upon to help writers who must edit their own work.

In any event, your responsibilities as an editor are threefold.

Act as the reader's advocate.   Your primary responsibility is to stand in place of the reader. This means applying the principles of good communication so that the package you hand the reader makes sense and is easy to read. The writer has, presumably, already tried to do these things. Your job now is to provide the final polish.

Provide a service to the author.   The language is complex. We have over half a million words that we can use and an endless number of ways of arranging them. An author who is language-wise realizes that no one person can do it all. Thus an editor provides a service to the author in much the same manner that engineers check each other's calculations.

Operate economically.   If you work for private business, you are obliged to make money. If you work for the taxpayers, you are obliged to save money. Either way, your responsibilities are to operate economically and to keep manuscripts moving. It also means managing your editing by assigning *levels of edit.* Levels of edit can be contrasted in this short statement: You would not edit a memo for the files in the same depth that you would edit a report going out to the public. Besides assigning levels of edit, you can also reject manuscripts that are uneditable. Editing time is expensive, and manuscripts that need total rebuilding should be returned to the author along with suggestions for revision.

The editorial process outlined below is a foundation on which you can develop your own methods.

1. Make sure you have all the pages.

2. Read through the manuscript and check for *substance,* that is, content, format, and policy. You should be asking questions like these:

Content: Does the document cover the ground? Are the conclusions justified? What is lacking? Has too much been provided? Does another publication already handle this topic?

Format: Is this the best way to present this information to the reader?

Policy: Are required parts of the manuscript present and prepared according to the organization's guidelines? Are disclaimers and distribution lists present as required? Does anything in the manuscript advertise or promote a competitor? Are any statements derogatory, libelous, or slanderous? Can we put this out to the public?

As you perform this first reading, take notes on a separate pad. The notes will help you in discussing the manuscript with the author.

If you detect any serious problems of substance, sit down with the author. Explain where the problems are, and have the author make the changes. If you as an editor make major changes and get in the habit of it, you will get a reputation for it. Your writers will then write less, and you will write more.

3. After problems of substance have been resolved, go through the manuscript again and correct problems of *mechanics.* Mechanics are all the details of punctuation, capitalization, transitions, parallelism, verb and noun agreement, verb tense, deletions, and on and on. Editing for mechanics is probably the most time consuming of all editorial tasks. It will be especially time consuming if you have to check many facts such as dates and names of people, places, and organizations.·

When correcting the mechanics of a manuscript, keep in mind that there are two kinds of style, an author's *personal style* and a *house style* (also called a *press style*). A house style is the way an editor or publisher handles such routine matters as capitalization, headings, and punctuation. A house style exists to save editing time and to make the mechanics of a publication consistent. A personal style is a writer's own unique way of writing. A good editor will recognize and respect the difference between styles.

4. Go through the manuscript again? You might, just to check your own work. But otherwise, what do you think will be gained? For one thing, you will use more of your time, and your time is worth money. Second, you will have to be especially alert that your style does not take the place of the author's style.

5. Discuss your changes with the author. Give a reason for changes. Explain the principles involved. If you edit by ear, read your corrections out loud. Better still, have the author read the *before* and the *after* versions out loud. Use the editing session as a low-key teaching session.

If you send a manuscript back with written comments, avoid cryptic terms like "needs work," "develop," or "fill out." Explain your requests. The author may see the problem differently than you do, and you may get a kind of "work," "development," or "filling" that is not what you wanted.

When working with authors, have something good to say about the manuscript. Writing is hard work, and authors like recognition. But if you cannot find something good to say, then you have a management problem, not an editing one, and the author may be out looking for a new job.

6. Plan time for extraordinary editing tasks. Extraordinary editing tasks may include some or all of the following: checking quotations against sources, doing or crosschecking research, writing missing sections, editing copy provided by a writer whose native language is not English, editing tapes, editing handwritten material, incorporating repeated changes to a manuscript, working with more than one author on a single manuscript, and dealing with out-of-town authors.

7. Finish the product. If you are dealing with a manuscript that will be typed, your job is almost over. If you want your product printed, find an established commercial printer. Work with the printer. Tell what you know about printing and production processes, and admit what you don't know. Ask for samples of the printer's work. Find out how long it takes to get work

done. Ask for suggestions as to type styles, paper, and binding. An hour talking to a good printer is equal to reading several books on what has become a complex and sophisticated process.

V.

HELP WITH SPECIAL PROBLEMS

If you wou'd not be forgotten
As soon as you are dead and rotten,
Either write things worth reading,
Or do things worth the writing.

> Benjamin Franklin
> (*Poor Richard's Almanac*)

VISUAL AIDS

A visual aid can be as simple as a two-column table or as intricate as the illustrations in *Scientific American*. In between are all types of charts, graphs, drawings, diagrams, and photographs. Many of these visuals are produced by graphic artists. Others, such as tables, can be set up by a typist. In no way, however, are you as writer left out.

To begin with, you will be expected to analyze your text for the purpose of suggesting uses and topics for visuals. If you are working with a graphic artist, you may have to provide rough sketches. If you are having a table typed, you will have to give the typist a handmade version to work from. In a low-budget operation, you may have to produce many of your own visuals. Regardless, it's your responsibility to see that the finished visuals work and that they are clear, correct, and integrated into the text.

A note of caution: The field of visual aids is broad. To make the topic manageable here, I have limited it to describing visuals that can be made by persons possessing little or no training in graphic arts. For more information on planning and using visuals, I strongly urge you to consult the references listed at the end of this book.

USING VISUALS

Pros and cons. Terms gathered from a variety of texts tell us that visual aids are emphatic, commanding, dynamic, convincing, and appealing; that visual aids add variety, are good for presenting summaries, and are compact ways of showing facts, figures, and statistics; and that visual aids are excellent for simplifying complex ideas. In addition, well-executed visual aids that present data in an orderly fashion allow the reader to grasp a lot of data easily and quickly. Furthermore, visuals are sometimes the only means by which some concepts can be presented.

But before you use any visuals, consider these thoughts. First, too many visuals or visuals that are too complex can overwhelm the reader. Second, it is difficult to quote from a visual: Far more than a thousand words may be needed to describe one picture. Third, visuals can be revealing: An unretouched photograph shows all—good and bad, significant and insignificant. Fourth, the appeal of visuals is subjective: Some readers are addicted to visuals, and others ignore them altogether.

Of course, the ultimate consideration is cost. Graphic art supplies and the services of a graphic artist are expensive, and the price of printing in color may be prohibitive.

Planning visuals. Despite these criticisms, we return to the starting point: Visual aids can do everything advertised for them. Therefore, here's a list of pointers that will help make visual aids work for you.

1. Use a minimum number of visuals. Pick only those visuals that (a) save long, involved explanations and (b) help the reader understand the text.

2. Make the illustration the smallest size required to portray clearly the desired information. At the same time make certain that everything will be legible if the illustration must be reduced for publication.

3. Try to design all visuals in a series so that all words, lines, and other elements will end up in a uniform size on publication.

4. Make the terms used in the visuals consistent with terms used in the text.

5. Don't try to be fancy. I once took part in a classroom experiment in which the participants were given 10 minutes to walk past a table on which over 30 different visuals were displayed. No specific instructions were given. All we were told was, "Just go in there and take a look." At the end of the 10 minutes we were asked which visuals we remembered. The overwhelming majority remembered, and liked, the same two charts. Both were simple to the point of being bare. Both were black and white, both contained a minimum amount of factual

information, both had considerable white space, and both were free of distractions.

In short, treat visuals the same as words: Use few and keep them simple.

Integrating visuals into the text. A visual aid should be put as close as possible to where it's first mentioned in the text. An exception is made for what are sometimes called *supplemental* visuals or visuals containing raw data or field observations; these types of visuals are usually placed in appendixes.

When introducing a visual, what do you say about it?

1. Tell the reader the visual aid exists. Mention the visual aid early in the discussion so that the reader can refer to it while reading.

2. For the first citation, refer to the visual by number and title (short title will do). A reference to a visual in another part of the document should include the approximate location: "See Figure 3-1 in Chapter 3."

3. Don't refer to "the table below" or "the graph on the next page." When the manuscript is printed, the table may not be below, and the graph may be several pages over.

4. If the visuals are simple, comment on major points and omit discussing minor details.

5. If the visuals are complex, give instructions on reading and interpreting them.

6. If you have placed visuals in appendixes, you may want to inform your reader of that fact.

Numbering and titling visuals. Visual aids can be numbered straight through the document or by section or chapter. The latter method is easier to work with in case the manuscript is reorganized.

Titles for visual aids should be similar in tone and style to titles used for parts of the text. A title should give a general idea of what the visual is about. A headline style title (title containing a verb) can be used for visual aids. The technique can be seen in these samples:

STANDARD	HEADLINE
Wheat Production for the Last Ten Years	Wheat Production Increases over Last Decade

Can a visual aid stand alone? Some organizations require that a visual aid stand alone. That is, the visual must be comprehensible to the user who has that sheet and nothing else. Following this practice can result in visuals with long titles, captions, keys, headings, and footnotes. Sometimes, lengthy explanations must be provided on separate sheets. In short, the stand-alone concept is often difficult to put into practice and therefore should be avoided.

TABLES

A table has at least two columns, a title, and a number. The headings at the top of the columns are called *boxheads;* the far left column is known as the *stub.*

Stub arrangement. The listing in the stub should give the reader a pattern to follow. Three common patterns are alphabet-

TABLE V-A1

Private Liquid Asset Holdings, Nonfinancial Investors

In billions of dollars, except ratios. Averages of Dec. daily figures. Comprises holdings by households, nonfinancial business, State and local governments, and personal trust funds.

Item	1960	1965	1970	1975	1976	1977	1978
Total	387	559	769	1,289	1,422	1,589	1,771
Currency and deposits	306	451	633	1,055	1,193	1,327	1,452
Currency	29	36	49	74	81	89	98
Demand deposits	105	119	152	193	200	214	225
Time deposits	172	296	432	788	912	1,024	1,130
Commercial banks	70	125	199	360	417	459	505
Nonbank thrift institutions	102	170	233	428	495	565	624
Other liquid assets	81	108	136	235	229	262	319
Negotiable certificates of deposit	-	15	22	58	43	52	65
Open-market paper	3	8	21	43	48	56	84
U.S. short-term securities	32	36	42	66	66	77	89
U.S. savings bonds (E and H)	46	50	52	67	72	77	81
Ratios: Liquid assets to GNP[1]	76	78	76	80	80	80	80
Time deposits[2] to liquid assets	26	31	30	33	25	36	35

- Represents zero.   [1] GNP=Gross national product.   [2] Nonbank thrift institutions only.

Source: Board of Governors of the Federal Reserve System.

ical, chronological, or by classification. Items in the stub are usually not numbered.

Capitalization. Stub entries are capitalized in sentence form; that is, only the first word and proper nouns are capitalized. The same pattern is followed for words in the columns. Boxheads can be capitalized in sentence style or in the same style as the table's title.

TABLE V-A2

HOUSEHOLDS WITH TELEVISION SETS: 1974

| Item | Percent of households with— | | TV sets per 100 households | |
	1 or more sets	1 or more color sets	Black & white	Color
All households	94.4	59.4	82	67
White	94.8	62.2	81	70
Black	91.0	35.7	98	41
Spanish origin	93.1	47.1	83	51
In central cities	93.3	52.4	87	62
In suburban rings	95.7	67.5	86	77
Outside metro areas	94.0	55.0	74	60
With annual income of—				
Under $3,000	87.0	29.1	75	30
$3,000-$4,999	92.3	38.6	78	41
$5,000-$7,499	93.9	48.3	80	52
$7,500-$9,999	94.8	55.9	78	60
$10,000-$14,999	96.3	66.0	82	73
$15,000-$19,999	97.0	76.3	87	88
$20,000-$24,999	97.1	78.4	89	91
$25,000 and over	95.6	81.5	92	103

Source: U.S. Bureau of the Census, *Pocket Data Book: USA 1976* (Washington, D.C.: U.S. Government Printing Office, 1976), p. 319.

Alignment. In the columns, figures are aligned on the right, and symbols, such as commas, decimal points, and dollar, percent, plus, and minus signs, are aligned vertically. Rows are aligned horizontally.

Abbreviations and devices. To save space, omit periods and use standard abbreviations and symbols. Unusual or new devices can be explained in a note. Avoid using ditto marks.

Rules (lines). The lines between elements are called *rules*. Horizontal rules are easy to do on a typewriter, but vertical rules take more time and effort. A way to resolve this problem is to rule tables only if spacing will not provide enough separation.

Showing totals. The traditional way to show a total is to place it at the bottom of a column of figures. Another way, which is of more help to the reader in a hurry, is to place totals at the tops of columns.

Continued tables. When a table is continued to another page, it is not necessary to repeat the title. Headings are repeated, and the table number is continued in this manner:

Table 4—continued

Citations and notes. The source of a table can be cited in the title (usually in parentheses) or at the bottom of a table in a note. Explanatory notes are usually placed at the bottom.

Two tables are shown here. The samples show many of the features mentioned above. In addition, Table V-A2 shows how to handle more than one degree of indentation in the stub.

LISTS

A list is a cross between straight prose and the simplest of tables.

The easiest type of list to construct is one like this: Our objectives for the coming year are to (1) increase efficiency, (2) improve quality, and (3) train new employees.

If you are writing a list made up of long items or if you want to make items more visible, however, you can arrange them in a vertical list. A vertical list is commonly introduced with a colon. Then numbers or typographical ornaments are used to call attention to the items:

1. Numbers are frequently used when steps must be described or performed in order. Care should be taken to prevent the lists' numbers from conflicting with the numbers assigned to headings. The usual way of preventing such a conflict is to type the heading numbers without parentheses and the list numbers in parentheses. The use of letters to set up a sequence should be avoided whenever possible. Which step is *h?* Seventh?

Ninth? Eighth? Readers will find it easier to follow a numerical sequence.

The double hyphen is easily done on a typewriter and is preferred over a single hyphen (-) or a period centered on the line (·). Both the single hyphen and the centered period are a little too weak to be used with a list, and a list is not a weak way of displaying information.

A "bullet," as shown here, is nothing more than a fat period. In the absence of special typesetting equipment, the bullet can be placed by use of a template, the typed small *o* filled in, or with transfer characters such as those sold by graphic arts suppliers. In most applications, the bullet is about the same size as a lowercase letter of the type style used in the list.

Note that a small amount of white space separates each number or ornament from the first letter of the line.

Note also that a capital letter begins the first line of each item in a list.

As for punctuation, the standard practices apply, with one exception: Short elements like the ones shown below need no ending punctuation when arranged vertically:

• Phrases
• Dependent clauses
• Rows of numbers
• Formulas

Also, lists with short items are usually indented. However, if items in a list are long, space can be saved by not indenting.

CHARTS

Charts are more difficult to construct than tables and lists but offer more variety and more visual impact. Many types of charts exist, but the ones examined here are some of those most frequently used and most easily understood by the reader. In addition, these charts were selected because they can be prepared by someone who does not have extensive training in graphic arts.

The method is as follows. A nonreproducing pencil was used to rough-in each chart on nonreproducing graph paper. The light blue of this type pencil and paper will "drop out" when the chart is photographed for reproduction. Then, if you do not want to use pens, you can cut tones, lines, and letters from sheets and place them on the graph paper. The sheets containing tones, lines, and letters are available at graphic art supply stores.

If you decide to produce your own visuals, you will find the following gadgets helpful: a triangle or T square, rubber cement, art-gum eraser, scissors, and an X-acto knife. Artists' supply stores stock these items and are great sources of advice and encouragement. Otherwise, the principal requirements are steady hands and patience.

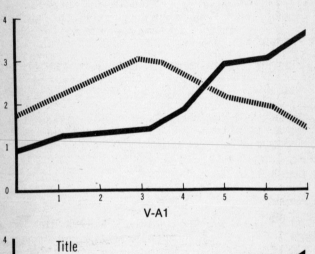

V-A1

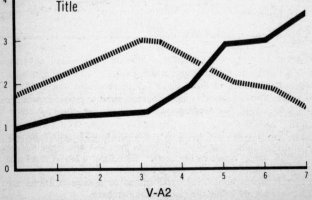

V-A2

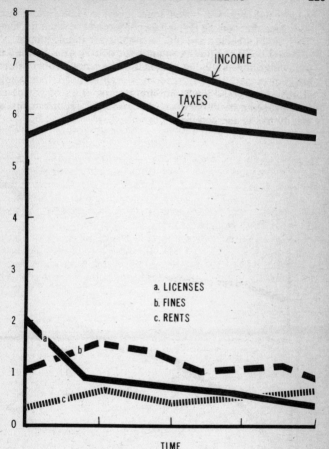

TIME

V-A3

Explanatory notes:
1. The top two lines are far enough apart to provide space for *labels*. For reading ease, the labels are placed horizontally.
2. Because the bottom three lines are close together, the use of labels would add clutter to the chart and leave a large empty space in the center. Therefore, a *key* is used and placed to provide visual balance.
3. Notes containing explanations or source citations are placed below the chart, as shown here.

Concerning the actual design—

1. Charts are usually laid out as oblongs. Scales of 4:3 or 7:4 are common. As an example, a chart can be laid out with a horizontal scale of 7 inches and a vertical scale of 4. When the chart is finished, it can be photographically reduced to fit the page.

2. The title has the largest lettering. The title and the chart number usually go above the chart. An exception can be made when better visual balance is possible by placing the title and number at the side or in a corner of the chart (Figures V-A1 and V-A2).

3. Label curves, bars, or columns on the chart, and place labels horizontally. Boxing of labels should be avoided; it's extra work and a distraction. When a key is necessary, it should be placed where it will balance other elements of the chart. Notes containing explanations or source citations are placed below the chart (Figure V-A3).

4. Many charted values have zero as a reference. When zero is the reference, show it; to do otherwise is to cheat the reader (Figures V-A4 and V-A5). On the other hand, a zero base line is not necessary when another reference, such as a cost-of-living index, is used.

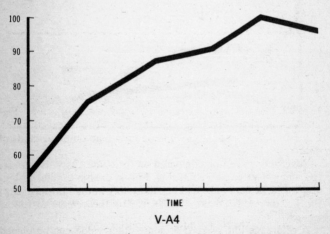

TIME

V-A4

5. When working with tints or tones, use a difference of at least 30 percent in shading between adjacent tones. The sheets the tones come on are labeled as to percent of darkness.

6. Avoid extreme contrasts of diagonals and straight lines; otherwise, optical illusions may result.

7. Before submitting your visuals to a printer, make a photocopy of your work and examine it critically. Looking at a photo of your visual aid is like reading your prose aloud. The flaws show.

Onward. The look at visual aids here begins with the question, What do I want to show—trends, wholes, or parts? A selection of charts is provided that will help answer that question.

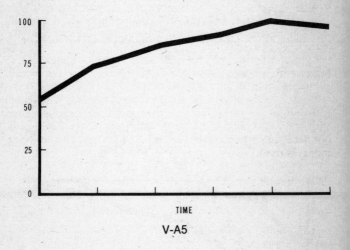

V-A5

To accent a trend. To accent a trend, use a *line* chart (Figure V-A6). Line charts also lend themselves to forecasts, interpolation, and extrapolation more readily than do other kinds of charts.

Several lines can be compared on the same chart. However, too many lines can be confusing. For an example, refer to Figure V-A3. If that figure had one more line in the bottom group, the clutter would make it difficult for the reader to follow trends.

A reference line of zero or some other value can be placed elsewhere than at the bottom (Figure V-A7).

To dramatize the trend, the curve can be filled in (Figure V-A8).

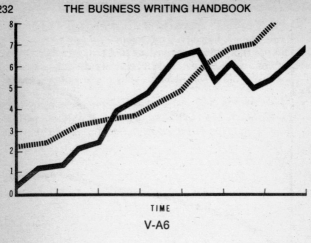

TIME

V-A6

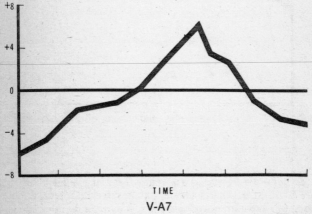

TIME

V-A7

When designing a line chart, the lines (curves) have the widest line, two times wider than the axes, and three times wider than any grid lines. Each curve should be the same width as the others.

To emphasize differences. Differences between sets of data over a period of time can be emphasized by use of a *column* chart (Figure V-A9). A column chart should not be used to emphasize a trend; a line chart is much better at this.

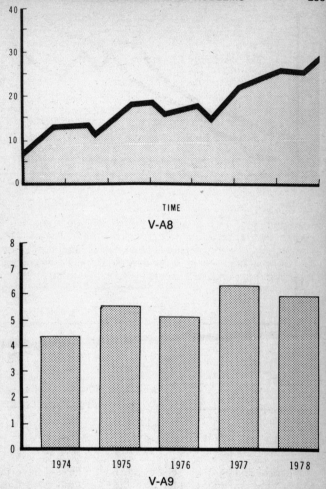

V-A8

V-A9

Differences between sets of data at one time can be emphasized by use of a *bar* chart (Figure V-A10). The bars must be arranged in some logical sequence, such as alphabetical, geographical, or numerical. Bars can also be arranged according to size, biggest bar at the top (or bottom), others stacked in order of decreasing length.

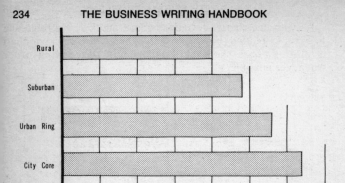

V-A10

Columns or bars can be grouped to compare a number of items in two, or three, respects (Figure V-A11). The comparison of more than three items can be confusing. The most important bar or column should be the darkest and in strong contrast to adjacent tones. All bars should be the same width. When the chart has many bars, the spaces between bars may be eliminated.

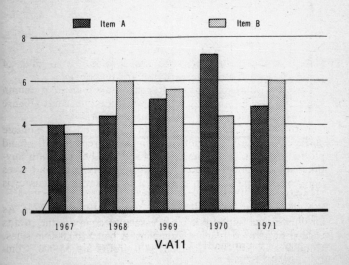

V-A11

As with line charts, deviations above and below a reference line can be plotted (Figure V-A12). When a deviation bar chart is plotted, bars should be arranged in descending order whenever possible.

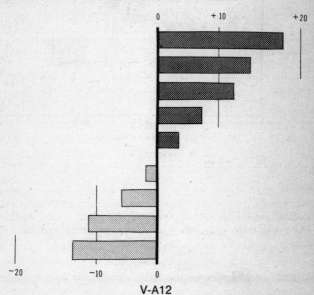

V-A12

To compare values of parts and wholes. Two kinds of comparisons can be made: absolute and percentage.

Absolute values can be compared on a *subdivided* column chart (Figure V-A13) or a *multiple surface line* chart (Figure V-A14). Subdivided bar charts can also be drawn.

With subdivided bar and column charts and with multiple surface line charts, the width of each band is read from the band plotted below it. Only the lowest band can be read with anything approaching accuracy. Therefore, this type of chart gives only a general picture and should not be used where accuracy is important.

Sometimes, it is not feasible to compare absolute values. As an illustration, suppose it is necessary to compare the profits earned by two companies. Company A had $100,000 in sales, Company B, $10,000. Company A's profits are $5,000, Com-

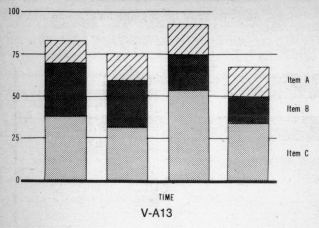

V-A13

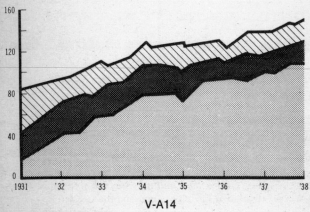

V-A14

pany B's, $600. The absolute differences are large. It would be difficult to construct a chart that would not leave the impression that something is wrong with Company B. A chart showing percentages, however, would give a truer picture. The chart would show that Company B earned profits at a six percent rate; Company A, at a five percent rate. Charts of this type are known as *100 percent* charts and can be constructed of the bar, column, or surface types.

A 100 percent bar chart is shown in Figure V-A15. Lines

connecting the segments guide the eye and make comparison easier.

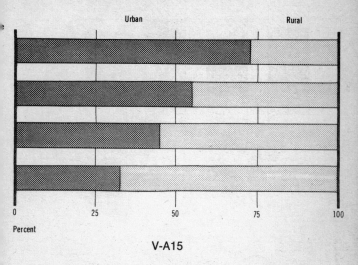

V-A15

A 100 percent surface chart is shown in Figure V-A17.

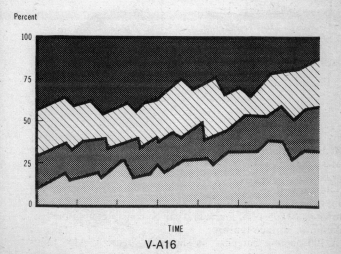

V-A16

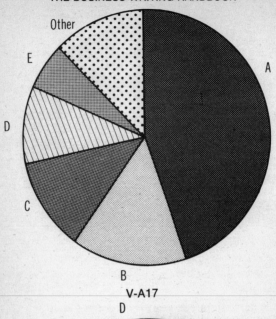

V-A17

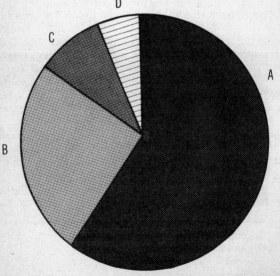

V-A18A

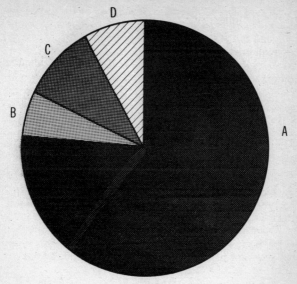

V-A18B

Percentages can also be compared by use of a *pie* chart (Figure V-A17). In a pie chart, sectors are arranged clockwise according to size. The largest sector begins at "high noon"; progressively smaller sectors follow. Whenever a segment labeled "other" is used, it is placed last. Avoid small segments (under 7 to 10 degrees), and try to limit the number of segments to five. If you wish to compare many segments, use a table. A particular advantage of the pie chart is that in being round it provides visual relief from long lines of horizontal type.

When two or more pie charts are compared, keep segments in the same order, regardless of size (Figure V-A18). This makes it easier for the reader to compare values.

For constructing a pie chart, some percentage values of a circle are:

360	degrees =	100 percent
180	degrees =	50 percent
90	degrees =	25 percent
36	degrees =	10 percent
18	degrees =	5 percent
3.6	degrees =	1 percent

As was stated earlier, the coverage of visual aids is limited here, and a reminder is given again to consult the sources listed at the end of the book. In addition, study critically the visuals you encounter in your reading. Analyze the quality of the artwork involved, and try to imagine if the visual couldn't have been presented better in a different form.

FORMS

Here is a short checklist that will help you plan and design forms.

Planning.

1. Establish the purpose of the form. Begin by finding out what programs the form will be associated with. Talk to the program managers. Find out why the form is needed.

2. Determine the content of the form. Talk to the people who will fill in the form and those who will read the form. Find out what bits and pieces of information the form is supposed to collect. Make a list of these points.

3. See that no other form already exists to do the job.

4. Try redesigning a similar form or updating an old one.

5. Consider buying the form. Buying forms from an office supply store may be the answer when you can get by with standard types.

Designing.

1. Arrange items for best use. The form's title, subtitle, and most important items should go at the top where they will be the most prominent. (Figure V-A19 can be referred to during the reading of these steps.)

2. Group items logically. Logical groupings save time when filling out the form and when extracting information.

3. Use lines to block off groups of information. Thicker lines can be drawn around mandatory or most important items.

4. Use arrows and other obvious visual signals to direct attention to particular items.

5. Determine the size of the form. Match the size to filing requirements and to other forms in the same category. Letter size (8½ x 11) is usually the most practical.

6. Strive for a good visual balance so that the form will be pleasing to look at.

7. Leave adequate margins so that the form can be bound or three-hole punched if necessary.

Title	Instruction block		File data

First priority answers

	Yes	No
Question 1	☐	☐
Question 2	☐	☐

Second priority answers

	Yes	No
Question 1	☐	☐
Question 2	☐	☐

Additional answers	Always	Sometimes	Never
Question 1			
Question 2			
Question 3			

Explanations of answers _____

Person completing form _____ last name   first   middle initial

Address _____ number   street

_____ city   state   zip code   Phone ( ) -

Signature _____   Date

V-A19

8. Give the form a number, a printing date, and a filing data block. The filing data block usually goes in the upper right corner.

9. Give instructions in simple and clear language. If instructions aren't clear, the form stands a good chance of being filled out incorrectly. Place instructions as close as possible to the item that needs explanation. Instructions on the back of a form can be overlooked.

10. Preprint information that is the same for all users.

11. As much as possible, request information that can be answered either *yes* or *no,* by checking a box, or by circling a word or letter. If an *either-or* choice is not possible, try designing questions that call for best out of three choices (such as *always, sometimes,* or *never*) or best out of five (such as *excellent, good, average, poor, unsatisfactory*).

12. Leave ample space for written answers. If you expect the form to be filled out on a typewriter, allow one inch for six lines of type. If you expect handwritten answers, allow room so that writing will not be cramped and illegible.

V-B.

NONDISCRIMINATORY WRITING

Language shapes thought. If language didn't shape thought, words like *propaganda* and *publicity* wouldn't be in dictionaries. If language didn't shape thought, politicians wouldn't be elected. If language didn't shape thought, Hitler would never have gotten out of the beer halls.

In shaping thought, language has the power to reinforce and perpetuate ethnic, racial, or sexual discrimination. Language used in this manner works against attempts to achieve equal opportunity in education, housing, and jobs; and equal opportunity is a national philosophy supported by law.

Discrimination in writing can be traced in part to the myths and stereotypes that have become associated with certain groups. This association has produced a form of folklore in which Italians are swarthy, Chinese are smiling and serene, blacks are athletic and shuffling, Mexicans are lazy, Spaniards are passionate, and native American Indians are proud and stoic.

Another form of folklore leads to discrimination on the basis of sex. This form stresses the concepts of male superiority and female inferiority. In this particular folklore, all positions of leadership are held by men, and all low-status occupations and activities are performed by women.

It would take a book larger than this one to trace the source of such attitudes. Still, we cannot deny their existence, and they do find their way into writing. A personnel report that evaluates Mary Smith as "a well-groomed black clerk" implies that other blacks are not well-groomed. An ad for a manager that reads "he is required to monitor production and he must act decisively" carries with it the message that only a man can handle the job.

In reality, attitudes such as these deny the fact that all sorts of personal attributes can be found in all groups and individuals. Therefore—don't label. All Asians are not inscrutable. All Anglo-Saxons are not poised and prim. All Scots are not thrifty. Many elderly people detest being called *senior citizens*. There is no such person as a *typical teenager*. All women are not weak and flighty, and all men are not strong, logical thinkers. A man's wife is not his *little woman*, and females in college are not *coeds;* they are students.

Another cause of discrimination in writing is found in the noun *man* and the pronouns *he, him,* and *his*. These traditionally have been used to apply to both men and women. Thus, we see statements like "Man works to protect nature"; "The manager is a busy person, and he needs the essential details of a report quickly"; and "An employee is encouraged to express his opinions about morale."

Granted, the writers of sentences such as these may not mean to exclude women. Still, the words literally say "men only," and the writing can be judged as discriminatory.

What is needed is a neutral noun or pronoun that applies equally to both sexes. The English language does not have such a word, but other alternatives are to:

1. Use the male noun *man* and the male pronouns *he, him,* and *his* when discussing a specific man only and not to lump everybody together regardless of sex.

2. When discussing people without regard to sex, use the genderless *one,* words such as *person* or *individual,* or the second person *you, your,* or *yours*. Thus, "his position in the organization" becomes "one's position"; "this person's position"; or "your position."

You can also neuter prose with *the* in certain situations. As an example, instead of writing of an engineer using "his test meter" write "the test meter."

In some instances, plurals work out. Thus "a man's opportunity is unlimited" becomes "their opportunity is unlimited" or "these people have unlimited opportunity."

Still another method is to write *he or she* instead of just *he* when both sexes are being referred to. When this is done, "he must have the appropriate technical ability" becomes "he or she must have the appropriate technical ability." Alternating between *he* and *she* is not limited to single phrases but can be done from sentence to sentence, paragraph to paragraph, or chapter to chapter.

But using *he or she* consistently in a short publication or alternating between genders in the parts of a longer publication poses problems a writer must be aware of. First, the frequent use of *or* is a weakness in style. Second, the frequent use of *he or she* or *his or her* bounces the reader back and forth, and the bouncing is tiring. If you can use some of the other methods suggested here, your writing will be stronger and show more polish.

Also, remember that language is first a spoken tool and then a written one. What sounds good usually reads that way. Therefore, if we are going to preserve the strength of our language we will have to avoid unpronounceable combinations such as *he/she* or *s/he*. How does one pronounce those crisply? Try it out loud: "he slant she," "he or she," "he and she"; or "ess slant he," "she he"? Which is right? What is meant? What does it *sound like?*

3. To further reduce discrimination in writing, use nonsexual titles and references:

INSTEAD OF	WRITE
man-made	synthetic, artificial
manpower	workers, workforce
man-hours	working hours, staff hours
gentlemen's agreement	informal agreement
you and your wife	you and your spouse
chairman	chair
businessman	executive, entrepreneur
foreman	supervisor
salesman	sales agent

4. When using names and courtesy titles, refer to men and women equally:

INSTEAD OF	WRITE
Roger Smith and Miss Jones	Roger Smith and Sarah Jones
Mr. Smith and Sarah Jones	Mr. Smith and Miss Jones
Roger and Jones	Roger and Sarah

Along these same lines, if you are writing to a woman and if you don't know if she is a *Miss* or *Mrs.*, use *Ms*. *Ms*. is generally accepted as being the female equivalent to *Mr*. The rule is to address women by the same standards as one addresses men.

5. Lastly, don't get carried away. *Host* and *hostess* are usable; *adulterer* and *adulteress* are specific and correct; and *leading lady* and *leading man* are bonafide titles.

Also, don't write *Black* unless you are willing to give whites equal uppercase time.

And if you are writing to an addressee whose gender is unknown, your options are: *To whom it may concern, Dear Sales Director, Dear XYZ Company, Dear Sir or Madam,* or perhaps no salutation at all. In any event, a term like *Dear Gentlepeople* is strictly a last resort. A writer in an organization where I worked did that once and got this reply: "Dear Sir. In an oil field, there are no gentlepeople."

V-C.

THE WRITER AND THE LAW

The business writer directly encounters the law when dealing with copyrighted material and when writing about or quoting from the law.

COPYRIGHT

Copyright is the right granted by law to an author, composer, playwright, publisher, or distributor to exclusive publication, production, sale, or distribution of a literary, musical, dramatic, or artistic work. In the United States copyright protection is established by federal law. The law is contained in Section 101, Title 17 of the United States Code. This law was revised effective January 1, 1978, by Public Law 94-553, otherwise known as the copyright act or the copyright law. The discussion that follows is based on this revision.

What is copyrighted. Works that can be copyrighted include books, periodicals, films, tapes, unpublished manuscripts, and any other product of authorship that is fixed in any tangible medium of expression.

A work that is copyrighted should contain a notice made up of three elements: (1) the copyright symbol © (copyrighted phonorecords use the symbol ℗), the word *copyright,* or its abbreviation, *copr.*; (2) the name of the owner of the copyright; and (3) the year of first publication of the work.

What is not copyrighted. Works in the public domain are

not copyrighted. These include works on which the copyright has expired and works for which no copyright has ever existed. In this last category are works published by the United States Government.

But here a few words of caution must be issued. First, if you encounter a work on which the copyright seems to have expired, it is safest to assume that the copyright has been renewed. You should make this assumption whether the renewal date is specified in the copyright notice or not. Second, an uncopyrighted federal publication may contain copyrighted material that has been used with permission. Therefore, before you use any part of a federally published document, make sure the part you use has not been copyrighted. If the part has been copyrighted, a notice to that effect should appear with that part or in the front of the document.

Duration of copyright. Under the old law, copyright protection was for a first term of 28 years. One renewal of 28 years could be granted. For a few years while the new legislation was pending, Congress extended the second renewal beyond 28 years, and now the second term for everything in copyright prior to January 1, 1978, is 47 years.

Under the new law, copyright is for the life of the author plus 50 years. In the case of a work prepared by 2 or more authors, the term consists of the life of the last surviving author plus 50 years after that author's death.

For works made for hire (defined later), and for anonymous and pseudonymous works, the term is 75 years from publication or 100 years from creation, whichever is shorter.

The system of copyright renewal that applied under the old law was not written into the new law for new works. However, the new law does contain language that affects copyrights granted under the previous law. These copyrights have been placed into two groups:

1. Works first copyrighted before 1950 whose copyright was renewed before January 1, 1978. These older works have had their copyrights automatically extended to a total term of 75 years.
2. Works first copyrighted between January 1, 1950, and December 31, 1977. Copyrights in their first 28-year term on January 1, 1978, will have to be renewed in order to be protected for a second term. The renewal will extend the total period of copyright for these works to 75 years.

The doctrine of fair use.   Fair use is the privilege an author has to use the work of another in a reasonable manner without having to ask permission of the copyright owner. In Section 107 of the copyright law, fair use is defined this way:

> The fair use of a copyrighted work . . . is not an infringement of copyright. In determining whether the use made of a work in any particular case is a fair use the factors to be considered shall include—
>
> (1) the purpose and character of the use, including whether such use is of a commercial nature or is for non-profit educational purposes;
>
> (2) the nature of the copyrighted work;
>
> (3) the amount and substantiality of the portion used in relation to the copyrighted work as a whole; and
>
> (4) the effect of the use upon the potential market for or value of the copyrighted work.

How much can you use?   *Fair use* is a rule of reason. Common sense will tell you whether or not you have to ask permission. The quoting of one sentence from an article would not violate the doctrine of fair use. The use of the only chart that appeared in a three-page article might violate the doctrine of fair use. The quoting of a whole chapter from a book stands a good chance of violating the doctrine of fair use.

A lot depends on how you plan to use portions of the works of others. If your uses are planned for solely nonprofit purposes and pose no threat to the income of the author, you are probably not exceeding the doctrine of fair use. But if you plan to make money on what you use of others or if your use would deprive the copyright owner of substantial income, a court could find that you had violated the doctrine of fair use.

Giving credit and getting permission.   Always give credit to your sources. If you quote directly from the work of another, if you paraphrase another author's conclusions, or if you summarize someone else's research, name your source. A footnote, note, or in-text reference will do (see section V-D).

Although you do not need to get permission to quote or cite works that are not copyrighted, it is wise to contact the author and mention your intentions, for two reasons. First, it is a courtesy; authors take pride in their works and like to know how their writing is being used. Second, the author may have revised the work, may have later thoughts about it, or may provide you with an updated version.

As to copyrighted material, you need to get permission when you believe that the amount you want to use exceeds fair use. A letter such as shown below can be used.

Dear . . .

I am writing an article entitled ". . ." for submission to . . . . Would you grant me permission to use the following:

Figs. 1 and 2 on pages 11 and 12 of . . . .

The usual acknowledgments and a full reference to your book will be included. If you would like the credit line to take any special form, please let me know.

Would you please indicate your agreement by signing and returning one copy of this letter?

Sincerely,

I grant permission to reproduce the material specified above.

> Signed: ....
>
> (copyright-holder)
>
> Date: ....

Credit line: ....

Works made for hire.   "Works made for hire" is a category that was added as part of the new copyright act. Section 101 of the act tells us that "a 'work made for hire' is a work prepared by an employee within the scope of his or her employment." In other words, the writing you do for your boss is work made for hire. If the work is copyrighted, it is copyrighted in the name of your employer, not your name, unless there is a written agreement that says otherwise. Other categories of work may also be "for hire" but unless there is an actual employment situation, there must be a written agreement confirming the "per hire" status of the work.

For further information.   Copies of the copyright act are available free of charge from the

Copyright Office
Library of Congress
Washington, DC 20559

You can keep up to date on copyright by asking that office in writing to place you on its Copyright Office Mailing List.

THE LAW SAYS. . . .

When you write about a law, do you quote it or paraphrase it? I ask because it's popular these days to condemn legalese. But if you paraphrase laws and regulations as a rule, you may be asking for trouble. Here's an example, based on the California Education Code, Section 48226. The code reads like this:

> Any child who is blind or deaf or partially blind or deaf to an extent which renders him incapable of receiving instruction in the regular elementary or secondary schools, but whose mental condition is such as to permit application to study shall be exempted from the provisions of this chapter, only when he is resident of a city, city and county, or school district which does not maintain special classes for the admission of such pupils and when he may not be admitted to the State School for the Blind, or the State School for the Deaf, but he shall be exempted only upon the written approval of the superintendent of schools of the county.

A writer rewrote that bit of legalese into this:

> Statutory exemptions apply to children who, upon the written approval of the county superintendent of schools, are blind or deaf to an extent that renders them incapable of receiving instruction in the regular elementary or secondary schools.

Now, according to the bottom version, a child has to have the written permission of the county superintendent of schools to be blind or deaf. And that's not what is supposed to be meant at all! Furthermore, the bottom version is woefully incomplete as to the facts. Compare the two, and you'll see what I mean. You can be certain that an editor did something about it before it was sent out.

The only safe way to handle such a problem is to quote the law directly.

V-D.

DOCUMENTATION

This chapter presents guidance on taking notes, keeping a record of the sources (books, articles, newspapers) your notes are based on, and the writing of footnotes, bibliographies, and appendixes.

BIBLIOGRAPHY CARDS AND NOTE-TAKING

Bibliography cards. For each book, article, or other source, a bibliography card should be made up to show the minimum facts of publication. For a book, these facts are found on the front and back of the title page (Figures V-D1 and V-D2) and are

Who wrote the book: author or authors, editor or editors, or organization

Full title, including subtitle if there is one

Series, if any

Volume number, if any

Edition, if not original

City of publication

Publisher's name

Date of copyright

For an article from a periodical, the facts of publication are

Title ──

Technical Reporting

Edition number ── THIRD EDITION

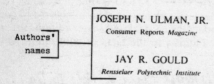

Authors' names ──

JOSEPH N. ULMAN, JR.
Consumer Reports *Magazine*

JAY R. GOULD
Rensselaer Polytechnic Institute

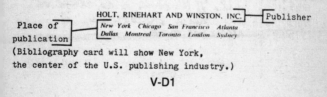

Place of publication ──

HOLT, RINEHART AND WINSTON, INC. ── Publisher
New York   Chicago   San Francisco   Atlanta
Dallas   Montreal   Toronto   London   Sydney

(Bibliography card will show New York,
the center of the U.S. publishing industry.)

V-D1

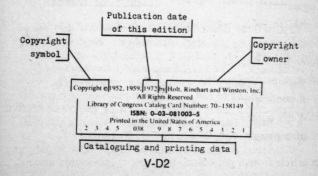

Copyright symbol

Publication date
of this edition

Copyright owner

Copyright © 1952, 1959, 1972 by Holt, Rinehart and Winston, Inc.
All Rights Reserved
Library of Congress Catalog Card Number: 70–158149
ISBN: 0-03-081003-5
Printed in the United States of America
2 3 4 5   038   9 8 7 6 5 4 3 2 1

Cataloguing and printing data

V-D2

Who wrote the article

Title of article

Name of periodical

Volume number, date, or both

Pages occupied by the article

Bibliography information is often kept on 3 x 5 cards, a convenient size to carry around and file. However, I have found it more practical to use 5 x 8 cards, for a couple of reasons. First, I double-space the facts of publication. This allows me to correct my mistakes or update the card if I find a later edition. Second, I add two items in addition to the facts of publication. One of

---

Davis, R.B., and Keller, Clara D. _How to Do Library Research_. 2nd ed. Urbana, Illinois: University of Illinois Press, 1975.

| State Lib. r2 1035.1 D68 1975 | A comprehensive guide to library reference sources. The bulk of the book is an extensive annotated bibliography of reference works. |

V-D3

Mills and Walter, Technical Writing

The authors characterize technical writing as (1) being about scientific and technical subjects, (2) having a scientific and technical vocabulary and conventional report forms, (3) possessing objectivity and impartiality, (4) conveying information accurately and concisely, and (5) concentrating on certain important writing techniques. The techniques are "description ... definition, classification, and interpretation" (pp. 4-5).

V-D4

these is where the publication is kept; if it's a library book, I also add the call number. The second item consists of my comments about the publication—the particular emphasis in the book or article, anything special that is included or omitted, and anything that I think is unique or helpful. All of these added notations help me evaluate the publication and find it when I want it again. A sample bibliography card used in preparing this book is shown in Figure V-D3.

Taking notes. Make sure that each quotation is copied correctly and that the source is listed with appropriate page numbers. As with bibliography cards, the 5 x 8 size can be used as shown in Figure V-D4.

DOCUMENTATION

Documentation can take the form of notes (and footnotes), a bibliography, or an appendix or appendixes. Sometimes all are used.

Notes. Notes are used to identify sources of quoted material. Notes are also used to show where you obtained facts and opinions other than your own. In addition, notes can be used to offer definitions necessary to an understanding of terms used in the text.

A note is called to the reader's attention by use of a number typed slightly above the line (a superior number or superscript). Notes are numbered consecutively throughout a chapter of a book or section of a report. Whenever possible, the superior number should come at the end of a sentence, for numbers set between words in a sentence distract the reader and break up the flow of information. Also, superior numbers that give the source of a quotation are placed at the end of the quote. The numbers follow all punctuation marks except the dash.

"This is all that was offered."[1]

(For the most recent trend, see the annual supplement.)[2]

Bernstein says so[3]—as do many others.

The notes themselves can be placed at the bottom of the page as footnotes or at the end of the chapter, section, or report. The note number is typed on the line and followed by a period. If notes are to be used as end-notes, they are typed double-spaced, and double-spacing separates each note. Footnotes for typewritten reports are typed single-spaced with double-spacing between each note. Footnotes on the bottom of a typed page should be separated from the text by the following: two blank lines and a solid line 15 spaces long beginning at the left margin. If type is to be set by a printer, footnotes are typed separately from the text, and the printer will place the notes on the bottom of the page. Some representative samples are shown here.

---

1. Seymour B. Sarason, *Work, Aging, and Social Change* (New York: Macmillan Publishing Company, 1977), p. 119.

2. Jorgen Holmboe, George E. Forsythe, and William Gustin, *Dynamic Meteorology* (New York: John Wiley and Sons, 1945), p. 53.

3. Ernest Erber, ed., *Urban Planning in Transition* (New York: Grossman Publishers, 1970), p. 7.

4. Federal Energy Administration, *National Energy Outlook, February 1976* (Washington, D.C.: U. S. Government Printing Office, n.d.), pp. 153-55.

5. Martin Gardner, "Mathematical Games," *Scientific American,* May 1978, pp. 24-30.

6. "Marshall Backs Labor Law Penalties on Employers," *Los Angeles Times,* May 22, 1978, p. 4.

7. Johnson to Smith, memorandum, March 2, 1976.

Footnotes and end-notes present advantages and disadvantages the writer should be aware of. Typewritten footnotes are extra work for the typist (or printer), who must carefully count lines and calculate page length to make certain that everything fits. Then too, a cluster of footnotes, even short ones, at the bottom of a page detracts from the appearance of a page. Also, both footnotes and end-notes cause breaks in continuity; the reader who stops reading text to check a note will have to make extra effort to pick up the thread upon returning to the text. In addition, end-notes carry with them the special problem of separating text from documentation, sometimes by several hundred pages.

An alternative is to give as much as possible of your documentation in the text itself. In-text documentation can make a page more readable and puts the source identification right next to the statement or quotation. A disadvantage of in-text documentation is that if the author uses too many sources in a paragraph or is not careful in arranging sources, the paragraph can become cluttered and difficult to read.

Examples of sources arranged for in-text documentation are given here:

> Paul G. Hewitt tells us "Albert Einstein was a slow child" (*Conceptual Physics: A New Introduction to Your Environment* [New York: Little, Brown and Company, 1971], p. 463). Representative statements are made in Norman Smith's "Roman Hydraulic Technology" (*Scientific American,* May 1978, p. 154). *Businessweek* (March 6, 1978, p. 26) establishes the cause of the dollar weakness as. . . .

Bibliographies. Bibliographies (sometimes called References, Sources, or Further Reading) give lists of works you have consulted. The bibliography is placed at the end of the text, either before or after the appendixes, and arranged alphabetically according to authors' last names. If a division into several groups seems desirable, authors should be listed alphabetically within a group. If no author is given, the title or editor's name can be used. Hanging indentation, as is shown below, is used.

Erber, Ernest, ed. *Urban Planning in Transition.* New York: Grossman Publishers, 1970.

Federal Energy Administration. *National Energy Outlook, February 1976.* Washington, D.C.: U. S. Government Printing Office, n.d.

Gardner, Martin. "Mathematical Games." *Scientific American,* May 1978, pp. 24-30.

Holmboe, Jorgen; Forsythe, George E.; and Gustin, William. *Dynamic Meteorology.* New York: John Wiley and Sons, 1945.

Johnson to Smith, memorandum, March 2, 1976.

"Marshall Backs Labor Law Penalties on Employees." *Los Angeles Times,* May 22, 1978, p. 4.

Sarason, Seymour B. *Work, Aging, and Social Change.* New York: Macmillan Publishing Company, 1977.

Note and bibliography style. You will make life easier for your reader if you avoid Latinisms in documentation and stick to English. In other words, don't use *ibid* (in the same place) or *op. cit.* (in the work cited). Instead, give the author's name, or short title of the work, and page: (Smith, p. 154) or (*Conceptual Physics*, p. 463). Also don't use *cf;* tell the reader to *compare,* or to *see,* or to *see also.* Other vague abbreviations are *ff,* for an indefinite number of pages following, and *et. seq.,* used to refer to an unspecified number of chapters or sections following. Tell the reader precisely what pages and parts of the document contain the information. Also, use *and others* in place of *et al.*

However, useful abbreviations are *p.* or *pp.* (for page or pages), *n.d.* (no date of publication given with document), and *n.p.* (no publisher's name given with the document).

Concerning underlining (or italics) or using quotation marks in notes and bibliographies, use these guidelines. For any document published by itself, underline its title. For any document published as part of a larger document, use quotation marks around the title of the part.

Appendix. An appendix is where you put material that needs to be in the document but is not an essential part of the text. Appendixes can contain detailed descriptions of equipment or procedures; calculations and detailed equations; discussions of methodology; worksheets, forms, laboratory reports; and copies of contracts. Each appendix is written as a separate unit and can be paginated with its own numbering system, such as A-1, A-2, A-3. Long appendixes can be published under separate cover.

V-E.

LIBRARY RESEARCH

The purpose of this section is to help you use the sources and services available in public libraries.

Card catalog. The card catalog is more than just a list of what books are in the library and where they're kept. For instance, a book's card tells how many pages are in a book; the page count gives some idea of how much detailed information is in the book. The card also gives the date of publication, which indicates how current the book is. Also, a book's card tells whether the book is illustrated. In addition, other cards in the card catalog give titles of periodicals (magazines or journals) shelved in the library.

Finding special words and terms. Libraries shelve dictionaries of many languages in addition to English. Libraries also contain dictionaries used in a number of specialized fields. Representative titles are:

Aviation and Space Dictionary. Defines terms used in aerospace sciences; illustrated.

Black's Law Dictionary. Defines legal terms and phrases including the principal terms of international, constitutional, and commercial law.

A Dictionary for Accountants. Defines and explains accounting terms and terms in related fields.

The Dictionary of Biological Sciences. Gives authoritative definitions of terms relating to the biological sciences.

Dictionary of Electronics and Nucleonics. Defines terms in electronics, nuclear and atomic science, radio, television, and computers.

Dictionary of Science and Technology. Provides comprehensive coverage in a number of subject areas; includes tables and charts.

Beginning research: the encyclopedia. An encyclopedia does not have enough space to go into great depth on any single topic. Still, encyclopedias do give a little information about many topics. For this reason, an encyclopedia is an excellent starting point. Two of the most frequently consulted are:

Encyclopaedia Britannica. Oldest, largest, and most famous of encyclopedias.
Encyclopedia Americana. One of the best of general encyclopedias.

An annual source of information: the almanac. Almanacs come out each year and contain useful collections of miscellaneous information. Three excellent ones are:

Information Please Almanac
New York Times Encyclopedic Almanac
World Almanac and Book of Facts

Finding out about places: the atlas. Atlases contain collections of maps and geographic information. Three leading atlases are:

Hammond Medallion World Atlas. Contains hundreds of political and topographic maps.
National Geographic Atlas of the World.
Rand-McNally Commercial Atlas and Marketing Guide. Chiefly an American atlas; emphasizes commercial aspects.

Finding out about people. Short biographies of prominent people are contained in these and other similar publications:

American Men and Women of Science. Covers living scientists in the physical and social sciences.
Dictionary of American Biography. The leading American biographical dictionary; excludes living persons.
Dictionary of National Biography. The leading British biographical dictionary; excludes living persons.
Who's Who in America. A biographical dictionary of notable living men and women. See also *Who's Who in the East, Who's Who in the Midwest, Who's Who in the*

South and Southwest, Who's Who in the West, and *Who's Who of American Women.*

Finding articles. If you want to see what articles are available on a topic, the place to look is the *periodical index.* Indexes such as are named here list journal, magazine, and newspaper articles by author or subject and sometimes both.

Applied Science and Technology Index. Indexes over 200 journals in a number of fields ranging from construction to electronics to physics and many others.

Business Periodicals Index.

Education Index.

Engineering Index.

Humanities Index.

Index to Legal Periodicals.

Index Medicus. Articles pertaining to medicine.

New York Times Index. A detailed index to daily issues of the *New York Times* only.

Reader's Guide to Periodical Literature. The most popular and perhaps the first place to look for any article.

Social Sciences Index.

Wall Street Journal Index. Indexes the *Wall Street Journal* only.

Finding books. If you are looking for a book on a subject, try:

Books in Print. Published annually; lists books still in print. (Note: The term *in print* means that the book is available for purchase. A book not "in print" may still be found in a library.)

Cumulative Book Index. Published annually; books listed may or may not still be in print.

Guide to Reference Books. A standard listing of books in a number of fields.

Finding government documents. Many of the publications of federal and state governments are kept in libraries. To the best of my knowledge, no single index exists for these publications. Some starting points are these four sources:

Government Reports Announcements.

Government Reports Index.

Monthly Catalog of United States Government Publications.

Monthly Checklist of State Publications.

For additional titles of government documents, look in the card catalog under subject headings like federal, Congressional, Census Bureau, and Department of Labor.

Looking up businesses.   Information about companies can be found in:

Standard and Poor's Register of Corporations, Directors, and Executives. Lists companies and products; gives brief biographies of executives.

Thomas' Register of American Manufacturers. Lists manufacturers by product and location; very complete listing.

City directories.

Telephone directories, especially the yellow pages.

Sources of statistics.   Statistical data are compiled in a number of publications. Among them are:

Demographic Yearbook. Gives various types of world population data.

Historical Statistics of the United States: Colonial Times to 1970. Gives a number of important statistics over the years; useful for making comparisons to current data.

Statistical Abstract of the United States. An annual compilation of statistics on population, immigration, finance, commerce, and more.

Using abstracts.   Abstracts are short summaries of scientific and scholarly works. By reading an abstract, you can often decide whether the entire document is worthy of further investigation. You can find abstracts in volumes with these titles:

Biological Abstracts.

Chemical Abstracts.

Computer Abstracts.

Dissertation Abstracts International.

Economic Abstracts.

Personnel Management Abstracts.

Physics Abstracts.

Other library services.   Other services that libraries offer include:

- Computer links to other libraries
- Interlibrary loan

- Microfilm and microfiche
- Pamphlet files (vertical files)
- Referral services to other libraries
- Telephone reference service

Miscellaneous sources.   Outside the library, miscellaneous sources of information include newspaper archives, local historical societies, libraries and archives operated by industries, government bodies, local colleges, and churches. Some of these facilities are available to the public; some aren't. A telephone call will tell you.

NOTES

Section I

1. Robert E. Heinemann, "Writing for Business: The Bucks Start Here," *Writer's Digest,* October 1977, p. 23.
2. *Writers at Work: The Paris Review Interviews, Second Series* (New York: The Viking Press, 1963), p. 219.

Section II

1. National Archives and Records Service, *Plain Letters* (Washington, D.C.: U. S. Government Printing Office, 1973), p. 39.
2. Clinton J. McGirr, "Guidelines for Abstracting," *Technical Communication,* Second Quarter, 1978, p. 2.
3. Oak Ridge National Laboratory, *The Growth of Electric Heating in the TVA Area* (Oak Ridge, Tennessee: Oak Ridge National Laboratory, 1977), p. v.
4. Paul R. McDonald, *Proposal Preparation Manual* (Covina, California: Procurement Associates, 1968), pp. II-6-10.
5. Robert K. Shnitzler, "Making Your Technical Proposals More Effective," Section 2, *Proposals and Their Preparation,* Anthology Series No. 1 (Washington, D.C.: Society for Technical Communication, 1973), p. 11.
6. Louis G. Juillard, "Proposal Evaluation in the Aerospace Industry," *Proposals and Their Preparation,* p. 25.
7. Robert K. Shnitzler, "Making Your Technical Proposals More Effective," Section 2, *Proposals and Their Preparation,* p. 13.
8. Jean Brodsky, ed., *The Proposal Writer's Swipe File* (Washington, D.C.: Taft Products, 1973), pp. 13-20.
9. Richard Nelson Bolles, *What Color is Your Parachute?* (Berkeley, California: Ten-Speed Press, 1978), pp. 11-12.
10. *IABC News,* January 1979, p. 7.
11. *World Book Encyclopedia,* Vol. 15 (Chicago: Field Enterprises Educational Corporation, 1969), p. 304.
12. Agricultural Research Service, *Environmental Aspects of Water*

Spreading for Ground-Water Recharge, Technical Bulletin No. 1568 (Washington, D.C.: United States Department of Agriculture, 1977), pp. 3-4.

13. *America's Handyman Book* (New York: Charles Scribner's Sons, 1961), pp. 1-2.

14. Agricultural Research Service, *Determination of the Compressive Characteristics of Lint Cotton with a Model Bale Press,* Technical Bulletin No. 1546 (Washington, D.C.: United States Department of Agriculture, 1976), pp. 2-3.

15. *America's Handyman Book* (New York: Charles Scribner's Sons, 1961), pp. 1-2.

Section III

1. U. S. Department of Health, Education and Welfare, *Fundamentals of Environmental Education,* April 1978 reprint (Washington, D.C.: U. S. Department of Health, Education and Welfare, 1976), np.

2. Theodore M. Bernstein, *The Careful Writer* (New York: Atheneum, 1973), p. 312.

3. George R. Klare, *The Measurement of Readability* (Ames, Iowa: Iowa State University Press, 1963), p. 171.

4. Carolyn Clark Reiley, "Can They Read What We Write," *Seminar,* September 1974, pp. 5-8.

5. Lewis Thomas, *The Lives of a Cell: Notes of a Biology Watcher,* (New York: Bantam Books, 1974), pp. 13-14.

6. United States Department of Agriculture, *The Gypsy Moth and Its Natural Enemies* (Washington, D.C.: U. S. Government Printing Office, 1975).

7. Donald H. Sanders, *Computers in Society,* 2d ed. (New York: McGraw-Hill Book Company, 1977), p. 391.

Section IV

1. U. S. Government Printing Office, *U. S. Government Printing Office Style Manual,* Revised ed. (Washington, D.C.: U. S. Government Printing Office, 1973), p. v.

APPENDIX: FURTHER READING

Editing aids.

O'Neill, Carl L., and Ruder, Avima. *The Complete Guide to Editorial Freelancing*. New York: Dodd, Mead, 1974.

United States Government Printing Office. *Style Manual*. Rev. ed. Washington, D.C.: United States Government Printing Office, 1973.

The University of Chicago Press. *A Manual of Style*. 12th ed., rev. Chicago: The University of Chicago Press, 1969.

Dictionaries.

The American Heritage Dictionary of the English Language. Boston: Houghton Mifflin Company, 1970.

The Random House Dictionary of the English Language. The unabridged edition. New York: Random House, 1967.

Webster's New Collegiate Dictionary. Springfield, Massachusetts: G. & C. Merriam Co., 1977.

Webster's New World Dictionary of the American Language. 2d college ed. New York: William Collins & World Publishing Co., 1974.

Webster's Third New International Dictionary of the English Language, Unabridged. Springfield, Massachusetts: G. & C. Merriam Co., 1971.

Language aids.

Bernstein, Theodore M. *The Careful Writer: A Modern Guide to English Usage*. New York: Atheneum, 1973.

Flesch, Rudolf. *The Art of Readable Writing*. 25th anniversary ed. New York: Harper and Row, 1974.

Follett, Wilson. *Modern American Usage: A Guide*. Edited and completed by Jacques Barzun and others. New York: Hill and Wang, 1966.

Fowler, H. W. *A Dictionary of Modern English Usage*. 2d ed. rev. by Sir Ernest Gowers. New York: Oxford University Press, 1965.

Gunning, Robert. *The Technique of Clear Writing*. Rev. ed. New York: McGraw-Hill Book Company, 1968.

Hayakawa, S. I. *Language in Thought and Action*. 3rd ed. New York: Harcourt, Brace Jovanovich, 1972.

O'Hayre, John. *Gobbledygook Has Gotta Go*. Washington, D.C.: United States Government Printing Office, 1975.

Strunk, William, Jr., and White, E. B. *The Elements of Style*. 2d ed. New York: Macmillan, 1972.

Letters, memos, and reports (including books that deal with technical writing).

Adelstein, Michael E. *Contemporary Business Writing*. New York: Random House, 1971.

Alred, Gerald J.: Brusaw, Charles T.: and Oliu, Walter E. *The Business Writer's Handbook*. New York: St. Martin's Press, 1976.

Brown, Leland. *Effective Business Report Writing*. 3rd ed. Englewood Cliffs, N.J.: Prentice-Hall, 1973.

Butterfield, William H. *Common Sense in Letter Writing*. Englewood Cliffs, N.J.: Prentice-Hall, 1963.

Comer, D. B., III, and Spillman, R. R. *Modern Technical and Industrial Reports*. New York: G. P. Putnam's Sons, 1962.

Douglass, P. F. *Communication Through Reports*. Englewood Cliffs, N.J.: Prentice-Hall, 1957.

Ewing, David W. *Writing for Results in Business, Government, and the Professions*. New York: John Wiley & Sons, 1974.

Fruehling, Rosemary T., and Bouchard, Sharon. *The Art of Writing Effective Letters*. New York: McGraw-Hill Book Company, 1972.

Janis, J. Harold. *Writing and Communication in Business*. 2d ed. New York: The Macmillan Company, 1973.

Mills, Gordon H., and Walter, John A. *Technical Writing*. 3rd ed. New York: Holt, Rinehart and Winston, 1970.

National Archives and Records Service. *Plain Letters*. Washington, D.C.: United States Government Printing Office, 1973.

Rathbone, Robert R. *Communicating Technical Information*. Reading, Massachusetts: Addison-Wesley Publishing Company, 1966.

Sherman, Theodore A., and Johnson, Simon. *Modern Technical Writing*. 3rd ed. Englewood Cliffs, N.J.: Prentice-Hall, 1975.

Ulman, Joseph N., Jr., and Gould, Jay R. *Technical Reporting*. 3rd ed. New York: Holt, Rinehart and Winston, 1972.

Uris, Auren. *Memos for Managers*. New York: Thomas Y. Crowell, 1975.

Library research.

Barzun, Jacques, and Graff, Henry E. *The Modern Researcher*. 3rd ed. New York: Harcourt, Brace Jovanovich, 1977.

Downs, R. B., and Keller, Clara D. *How to Do Library Research*. 2d ed. Urbana, Illinois: University of Illinois Press, 1975.

News releases.

Golden, Hal, and Hanson, Kitty. *The Techniques of Working with the Working Press*. Dobbs Ferry, N.Y.: Oceana Publications, 1962.

Ryan, Michael, and Tankard, James W., Jr. *Basic News Reporting*. Palo Alto, California: Mayfield Publishing Company, 1977.

Weiner, Richard. *Professional's Guide to Publicity*. New York: Richard Weiner, 1975.

Nondiscriminatory communication.

International Association of Business Communicators. *Without Bias: A Guidebook for Nondiscriminatory Communication*. San Francisco, California: International Association of Business Communicators, 1977.

Proposal writing.

Ammon-Wexler, J., and āp Carmel, Catherine. *How to Create a Winning Proposal*. Santa Cruz, California: Mercury Communications, 1976.

Hall, Mary. *Developing Skills in Proposal Writing*. Corvallis, Oregon: Oregon State System of Higher Education, 1971.

McDonald, Paul R. *Proposal Preparation Manual*. Covina, California: Procurement Associates, 1968.

Society for Technical Communication. *Proposals and Their Preparation*. Anthology Series No. 1. Washington, D.C.: Society for Technical Communication, 1973.

Taft Products. *The Proposal Writer's Swipe File*. Washington, D.C.: Taft Products, 1973.

Resumés and job-search help.

Boll, Carl R. *Executive Jobs Unlimited*. New York: Macmillan Publishing Company, 1965.

Bolles, Richard Nelson. *What Color is Your Parachute? A Practical Manual for Job-Hunters and Career Changers*. Berkeley, California: Ten Speed Press, 1978.

Lathrop, Richard. *Who's Hiring Who*. Berkeley, California: Ten Speed Press, 1977.

Visual aids.

Hoelscher, Randolph P.: Springer, Clifford B.: and Dobrovolny, Jerry S. *Graphics for Engineers: Visualizations, Communication, and Design*. New York: John Wiley and Sons, 1968.

Kaiser, Julius B. *Forms Design and Control*. New York: American Management Association, 1968.

Lockwood, Arthur. *Diagrams*. New York: Watson-Guptill, 1969.

Luzadder, Warren J. *Basic Graphics*. 2d ed. Englewood Cliffs, N.J.: Prentice-Hall, 1968.

Murgio, Matthew P. *Communications Graphics*. New York: Van Nostrand Reinhold Company, 1969.

Rogers, Anna C. *Graphic Charts Handbook*. Washington, D.C.: Public Affairs Press, 1961.

Spear, Mary Eleanor. *Practical Charting Techniques*. New York: McGraw-Hill Book Company, 1969.

INDEX

ABOUT THE AUTHOR

WILLIAM C. PAXSON is an editor and writer in Sacramento, California. His experience includes writing and editing articles, instructional texts, newsletters, and reports in a wide variety of fields such as air pollution, electronics, school administration, and travel. "Mainly," he says, "I have spent most of my professional career translating bureaucratic gobbledygook and scientific jargon into plain English." Mr. Paxson also teaches business and technical writing.